MAINLY ABOUT
WOLVES

British Library Cataloguing-in-Publication Data
A catalogue record for this book is available from the
British Library

Ernest Thompson Seton

Ernest Thompson Seton was born on 14th August 1860, in South Shields, County Durham, England. He grew up to be a pioneering author, wildlife artist, founder of the Woodcraft Indians, and one of the originators of the Boy Scouts of America (BSA).

The Seton family emigrated to Canada when Ernest was just six years old, and most of his childhood was consequently spent in Toronto. As a youth, he retreated to the woods to draw and study animals as a way of avoiding his abusive father – a practice which shaped the rest of his adult life. On his twenty-first birthday, Seton's father presented him with a bill for all the expenses connected with his childhood and youth, including the fee charged by the doctor who delivered him. He paid the bill, but never spoke to his father again.

Originally known as Ernest Evan Thompson, Ernest changed his name to Ernest Thompson Seton, believing that Seton had been an important name in his paternal line. He became successful as a writer, artist and naturalist, and moved to New York City to further his career. Seton later lived at 'Wyndygoul', an estate that he built in Cos Cob, a section of Greenwich, Connecticut. After experiencing vandalism by some local youths, Seton invited the young miscreants to his estate for a weekend, where he told them what he claimed were stories of the American Indians and of nature.

After this experience, he formed the Woodcraft Indians (an American youth programme) in 1902 and invited the local youth to join (at first just boys, but later girls as well). The stories that Seton told became a series of articles written for the *Ladies Home Journal*, and were eventually collected in *The Birch Bark Roll of the Woodcraft Indians* in 1906. Seton also met Scouting's founder, Lord Baden-Powell, in 1906. Baden-Powell had read Seton's book of stories, and was greatly intrigued by it. After the pair had met and shared ideas, Baden-Powell went on to found the Scouting movement worldwide, and Seton became vital in the foundation of the Boy Scouts of America (BSA) and was its first Chief Scout (from 1910 – 1915). Despite this large achievement, Seton quickly became embroiled in disputes with the BSA's other founders, Daniel Carter Beard and James E. West.

In addition to disputes about the content of Seton's contributions to the Boy Scout Handbook, conflicts also arose about the suffrage activities of his wife, Grace, and his British citizenship (it being *an American* organization). In his personal life, Seton was married twice. The first time was to Grace Gallatin in 1896, with whom he had one daughter, Ann (who later changed her name to Anya), and secondly to Julia M. Buttree, with whom he adopted an infant daughter, Beulah (who also changed her first name, to Dee). Alongside his work with the Woodcraft Indians and the BSA, Seton also found time to pursue his primary interest – that of nature writing.

Seton was an early pioneer of animal fiction writing, his most popular work being *Wild Animals I Have Known* (1898), which contains the story of his killing of the wolf Lobo. He later became involved in a literary debate known as the nature fakers controversy, after John Burroughs published an article in 1903 in the *Atlantic Monthly* attacking writers of sentimental animal stories. The controversy lasted for four years and included important

American environmental and political figures of the day, including President Theodore Roosevelt. Seton was also associated with the Santa Fe arts and literary community during the mid-1930s and early 1940s, which comprised a group of artists and authors including author and artist Alfred Morang, sculptor and potter Clem Hull, painter Georgia O'Keeffe, painter Randall Davey, painter Raymond Jonson, leader of the Transcendental Painters Group, and artist Eliseo Rodriguez.

In 1931, Seton became a United States citizen. He died on 23rd October, 1946 (aged eighty-six) in Seton Village in northern New Mexico. Seton was cremated in Albuquerque. In 1960, in honour of his 100th birthday and the 350th anniversary of Santa Fe, his daughter Dee and his grandson, Seton Cottier (son of Anya), in a fitting tribute to the man who loved his surrounding countryside so much, scattered his ashes over Seton Village from an airplane.

Ernest Thompson Seton

MAINLY ABOUT
WOLVES

Preface

MORE than half of this book is given over to stories of historic wolves ; for, of all wild beasts, the wolf had the largest share of interest among our Aryan ancestors of the days when men were groping for light and for leadership from savagery.

Throughout the early history of Europe, the wolves were a nightly terror to man and beast. They must have existed in thousands, if not by millions ; and, because they combined numbers with strength and cunning, there was no creature that could face and fight them with success.

High walls and nightly vigilance were imposed on all human dwellers of the land. The wild things had to seek safety in holes, in tall trees, in impenetrable thickets, on islands, or on inaccessible rocks that were easily defended.

But the wolfish toll went on. The fear of the wolf was on all the world without ceasing. Yet we find comparatively little mention of the wolf in history. Why ? Let us illustrate.

Chicago has, in its subsoil lurking-places and darker corners, millions of rats. Yet we see no daily mention of the fact in the current records.

It is well known and taken for granted ; their wastage is an annual and expected overhead. But when the rats are forced by fire or flood into open view, and in a desperate mob attack dogs and men, killing children and helpless things, then only is it that they come into notice. And a lurid paragraph is filed in every print house, setting forth details.

So with the wolves. In ordinary measure of destruction, they were accepted as inevitable ; but when a harder winter forced the wolves into larger, fiercer bands so they came into the open and devastated a town, then was there made historic record. Or when some wolf of giant size and superlupine cunning came upon the stage, then was a marvellous story full set forth, shocking, blood-curdling, never-to-be-forgotten ; then was a red, red chapter writ.

It would be easy to give the names of a score of these heroic wolves, and something of the lives they lived. Two at least there were whose appalling records won for them large space on the scroll of history—long chapters—red—unique. These two, I give at some length—' Courtaud, the King Wolf of France ' (A.D. 1430) ; and ' La Bête,

the Beast Wolf of Gevaudan' in South France
(A.D. 1764). Both of these belonged in the
man-eater class. While all the main outlines
of these two stories are historically correct, I
have embellished and expanded with the utmost
freedom.

'The Last of the Irish Wolves' is actual history.
The incident herein related is authentic, although
in telling it I have developed it somewhat. But
it seems beyond doubt that Rory Carragh, the
famous wolf-hunter, did, with the help of a small
boy, kill the two great wolves of Tyrone, as
related, about A.D. 1658. (See Sir James Ware,
Works, Dublin, 1764; also *Biography of a Tyrone
Family*, Belfast, 1829, p. 74.)

'Little Marie and the Wolves' in brief form
was recorded by the anonymous author of *Wolf
Hunting in Brittany* (1850). He gives it as actual
history; and it serves, in contrast with Courtaud,
to show how completely the modern wolves in
France had learned to respect human life.

The main thought in 'The Wolf and the Primal
Law' was suggested by several hunter tales. I saw
nothing of it personally, but have heard of many
similar cases. In bare outline, the final incident

was supplied by James R. Lowther, of Victoria, B.C. He guarantees its authenticity.

' Rincon, or the Call in the Night ' was, in its fundamentals, a personal experience ; but is expanded as fully as seemed helpful to the romance.

' The Wolf on the Running-board ' is told as it happened, without embellishment.

There was a time when the American wolf was, above all things, a creature of valour and speed. By these he lived, and had no fear of any other creature, however great its speed and valour.

But a mighty change came over the big buffalo wolves when the whiteman appeared on the scene, equipped with horses for speed and modern guns for destruction—a combination too strong for any beast, however valiant it might be.

These were the things that turned the fierce roistering buffalo wolves into creatures of cunning above all that live in the great broad West.

Those who know the wolf only as a hateful thing, a destroyer of stock, a bandit on the ranges, may be surprised and informed if they ponder the story of ' Wosca, the Cody Wolf ', which is founded

on well-authenticated incidents. My personal acquaintance with the fierce creature was limited to
one or two hunts after him near Medora, North
Dakota. But the episodes set forth are sponsored
by many men whose names will carry weight ;
though, of course, it is certain that not one, but
many different wolves, are compounded in the
central figure.

Valuable sidelight on this animal may be
obtained if we keep in mind the fact that a wolf
is simply a big, wild, but very doggy, dog, getting
his living by his wits and the strength of his jaws.
Wolves, like all highly specialized creatures, show
enormous individual variation, mental and physi-
cal ; most wolves are of heroic courage, yet I
have known of some who were utter poltroons
when facing dire extremity. Their personalities
are as diverse as saint and devil ; some are mentally
so low that we can but class them as morons, some
are gifted with cunning that makes them seem
endowed with genius of transcendent force.

This seems to be mostly a book of famous wolves.
It is so because my sympathies and my studies have
led me chiefly to that field. But the folksiness of

other creatures has been brought home to me in real life.

'The Story of Carrots' is fiction, with a basis of fact drawn from my own experience.

The same remark applies to 'Chicaree'.

'Hank and Jeff' is a traditional story of the Kentucky woods. I heard it when a child, and have told it many times by the camp-fire, but only recently put it on paper.

'The Chillingham Bull' was my personal experience in the north of England, 21 May, 1913; and is given without embellishment.

The peroration, 'Who Were the Heroes?' is rewritten from memory. I do not know where it is to be seen in print.

Those of you who would divide the world into human emotion and (on a far lower plane) animal impulse, have not dipped deep into the wells of truth. You have barely skimmed those stagnant ponds, those abysms of ignorance, called dictionaries and encyclopedias.

I wish I could take you out with me to sit by the camp-fires of the old-timers, to hear their blasphemous truths, to rake the gold out of their garbage bins, to learn the big things that come out of daily, nightly communion, but which are absolutely destroyed by creeds, by orthodoxies, as surely as the Copernican cosmogony was damned by the church folk of his day.

Contents

Illustrations

ET SETON

UNDISMAYED

POISON

POISON

An Appeal to Readers

or The White Mother Wolf

Our traditional picture of the wolf presents an odious creature, a monster of cruelty and destruction; actuated by nothing higher than a gluttonous appetite for food.

Yet I have seen wolves that were dainty as deer in matters of diet. I have learned of wolves whose master trait was wisdom.

I have known of wolves whose animating force was the spirit of adventure. I have been told of wolves whose strongest motivation was revenge.

I have met many a wolf whose overwhelming motive was the love of its little ones. I have seen wolves whose master passion was devotion to a dearly loved mate. I have heard of wolves who made a brotherhood pact, an affectionate alliance with some wholly different animal.

And I have knowledge of one wolf at least whose chiefest binding urge in life was loving devotion to his blind and helpless old mother.

Ye who would hear the tale as I got it from hunters

I   I

*and the sage-brush clan of the far North-west, listen now
to the story of Wosca and her valiant cub Shishoka.*

I

ABOUT 1890, there
lived in the valley of
the Little Missouri a
well-known white wolf, a female, a pest among
the cattle. Though not of large size or remarkable
speed, she was endowed with such superlupine cunning that she was known and feared from Sentinel
Butte to Palanata, and from Deadwood westerly to
Powder River—ten thousand square miles of the
finest cattle range in the West.

She never killed sheep or big steers ; but showed
a marked partiality for yearlings, preferably of the
blooded stock ; for about this time, the white-faced
Herefords were beginning to displace the old-time
longhorns of the range.

She was identified by her white colour, her
punched left ear, and the lack of the outside toe
on each front foot, whether a natural deformity or
the result of accident is not known.

Wolves pair for life, and commonly hunt in

2

couples—a good example of team play in perfect partnership.

The white wolf's mate was never identified, and it is believed that he was killed while she was yet young, and that thenceforth she lived alone except for the company of her latest brood.

Among the most impenetrable and forbidding of the Badlands west of the Little Missouri, a wolf hunter named Bud Dalhousie found a den of young wolves. He got a glimpse of one old one, the mother he believed ; but she was too shy to come near. She was nearly pure white ; and later, when he examined her track, he noted that there were but three pad-marks for each front foot, which settled her identity.

He crawled into the den, found five pups. Of these, he killed four, with a view to the bounties ; but saved one vigorous 'little rascal' for bait to catch the mother, or possibly both parents. This one was ashy grey like the others, but its head and face were washed over with a reddish ochre tint ; for which circumstance he called it the Red-headed Pup.

From the rocky lair down the gulch and over the fierce rifts which he crossed on foot, he left a trail

3

by dragging one of the dead pups. Then, having
got back to his horse, he trailed the body at the
end of his lariat to his ranch-house, some five long
rugged miles away.

There was not much left of the wolfling's body
when he got there, but enough to claim the five
dollar bounty.

Now he prepared for the inevitable visit that the
mother would make that night. A quarter-mile
from the ranch-house in a bare open spot with
clumps of Spanish bayonet, he prepared his trap.
On the neck of the red-topped pup, he put a collar
with a stout dog-chain, and fastened this to a stake
well driven in.

Just beyond reach of the chained pup, he buried
four strong wolf traps, buried them with the consummate art of an experienced trapper, buried them
so there was not the slightest hint of a buried trap
so far as the eye could detect. Then he threw bits
of cactus carelessly between the traps, leaving a
clear smooth place on and over each fateful pan.
No wolf will tread on cactus ; to shun that is an
early lesson in their training.

All was now set for the visit that the bereaved
mother would certainly make that night to rescue

her baby. Every precaution had been taken to make the snare succeed ; but there is one sense that the wolf has in perfection, and which it is nigh impossible to fool. That is, scent ; the scent of iron is very slight to us, but to the wolf it is as strong as it is fearsome. Even when hidden in the ground, and masked with diverse potent smells, the old wolf would surely smell the iron. But, on the other hand, the sight and smell of her little one would drive her to any desperate length, might make her throw all caution to the winds. And so it was.

The night wind was blowing starkly when the heart-hungry mother wolf came galloping down the trail that the wolver had laid. Craftily he had lulled suspicion by setting his bait and snare in the level open. The mother wolf approached up-wind. Her easy gallop slowed to a trot, to a walk as she came on the scene ; and the captive cub, sensing his mother's approach, raised his baby voice in a succession of vigorous squeals and whines.

Curbing her mother instinct to rush direct to him, she circled the place with nostrils near the ground. She made appraisal of every scent and object. The baby's chain was but six feet long, so that as he

5

circled round his stake, he was describing a twelve-foot ring, outside of which were the four great grim-jawed traps in perfect hiding, waiting, biding the time when they should do their work, and prove their mighty power.

But the scent of iron was there ; and, as the mother went around, she was thoroughly informing herself. Why the cub did not run to her was puzzling. But she could go to him.

With a long, quick bound, she covered the distance from her safe outer circle, over the hidden traps, into the safe inner circle by her cowering pup. She seized him as a she-wolf or a cat is wont to seize, by the scruff of the neck. But in this case, by good luck, the scruff was covered and protected by the leather collar. Setting off with the pup in her mouth, she meant to bound far away over the hidden menaces about her. She put her strength into that bound. But, at the end of the chain, she was stopped with a fearful jerk that threw her to the ground. It might have killed the pup ; but, luckily for him, the chain and collar bore the brunt, and the stake in the ground was so wrenched that on her second spring, the stake came up, and the mother wolf went off with the rescued little

6

one in her teeth and the chain and stake trailing after.

She went at her best speed for the three miles that covered the open plain. Then, reaching the coulées with their brushwood, she went more slowly ; and, in a sheltered place, lay down to nurse the pup. And much he needed it. Yet his joy in the solace of his belly-hunger was small compared with the joy she had in her heart-hungry consolation.

Here she left him for her nightly food quest. And here he was curled up alone, when with the sunrise came the wolver. He had gone forth at dawn to see the result of his trapping. The tell-tale footprints gave him all the record of the night ; and speedily he, with his trailing hound and some fighting dogs, was hard galloping on the track of the escaping mother and child.

They went direct to the hiding-place of the young pirate.

At the very same time, the mother was returning with a jack-rabbit in her jaws. The wolver's hand flew to his gun, a ball whizzed past the mother's head. She sprang over a near ridge and wholly disappeared.

Of one thing chiefly is the wolf afraid ; that is, guns, the thunder that kills from afar. Never will they face it. And the mother wolf was gone.

The dogs easily found the red wolf cub. He tried to run, but he still was bound with collar and chain, and these to a heavy stake which caught in the bushes, and held him so that Bud Dalhousie had no difficulty in retaking the cub.

In an hour, he was securely held in a chicken-wire cage at the ranch, and offered cow's milk and chicken heads, both of which he sulkily refused.

2

All attempts to capture the white wolf continued to be utter failures. Apparently she had lost track of where her little one was held ; or perhaps gave up as hopeless all plans of rescue.

She herself continued on the range. The yearling heifers, hamstrung and throat-cut, with one meal taken out of the ham, combined with the sinister track—two forefeet, each lacking a toe—and on one or two rare occasions in the firelight when a white wolf was seen with a punched left ear, all kept the world of cattlemen aware that the old white devil still was on their range.

Meanwhile, the red pup grew. Once he learned to lap milk from a pan and gorge himself on chicken heads and beef scraps, he grew apace. At three months, he gave promise of being a monster.

Then, one day came a-riding one Colonel Cody, better known as Buffalo Bill. And when he saw the big lubberly wolf pup with the auburn hair, he was possessed of a desire to own him that resulted in the wolver's collecting double bounty money ; and Bill went off with the pup.

On the Cody ranch, he continued for a year ; and it was here that an Indian scout dubbed him Shishoka, the Red-head.

During his ranch life, he learned many things that were vastly useful to him in his after life, and which could not have been learned on the open range : such as the comparative danger of man, woman, and child ; the unpleasant compulsion of a chain ; the value of lying low in a hollow when observation promised to be more helpful than escape ; the meaning of a turkey vulture making for a slaughter-house ; the message conveyed by a cowhorn blast ;

and above all, the deadly menace of the strychn
smell.

During this period, the red wolf had been k
on a chain, with a kennel for weather ; but
seemed so thoroughly dog-like and tame t.
Buffalo Bill decided to give him a larger meas
of liberty. One day, he unsnapped the chain fro
the wolf's collar, and let him run. The delight
freedom possessed the big wolf. He gambol
around like an overgrown puppy ; but was eas
decoyed within reach when meal-time came w
a big beef bone. Once or twice the experim
was repeated, but each time the wolf was har
to recapture. Then, one fine day, during
absence of the boss, the cook turned loose the
wolf, which quietly walked off, in spite of whist
and savoury meat invitations from the cook. A
that was the last seen of the Cody wolf in t
section of the West.

Under the urge of some inherited impulse,
travelled slowly northward, resting all day at tim
but ever northward, till at length, his sense of
home-ness was satisfied when once more he was
Butte County, Montana, with its dimly remen
bered buttes and rivers, its well-remembered sme

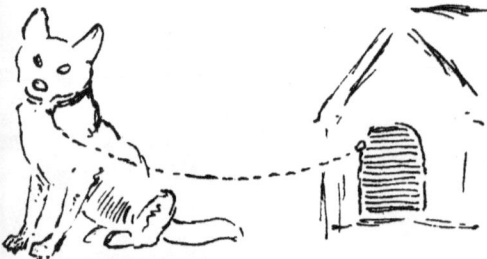

Vosca

3

All men who hunt or study wolves know that
they have the country marked at every mile or less
with some prominent object that serves as an
information bureau. It may be a conspicuous
boulder, a buffalo skull, a fence corner, or even a
clod where two trails cross. The tell-tale musk is
usually left at the place with the kidney product as
a medium. This musk varies with every individual,
and is quite distinctive ; while the foot scent of
the caller shows whence he came and whither he
went.

With such a system of signal and record, what
wonder is it that Shishoka, the Cody wolf, soon
found a kind companion. Whether he knew and
recognized his old mother is doubtful ; but certainly he accepted her as a hunting partner, and very
shortly afterwards, the night herders were made
aware that the white she-devil—Wosca in Indian
phrase—had hooked up with another wolf, a giant
with a reddish head and something on his neck that
looked ' powerful like a collar '.

Now there was a new and stronger combination
—her many years' experience and superlative cun-

ning, combined with his youth, strength, speed and knowledge of man's tricks when at home.

Yarns detailing their incredible sagacity were the theme of nightly fires. One of their tricks was wholly new to the ranchmen. The smaller wolf would sneak to a barnyard, and seize some noisy animal like a pig or a chicken, and hold it, loudly squealing, till all the dogs and men were headed that way on murder bent. Then, as their onset promised danger, she would release the victim, and disappear in the night, followed for a while by noisy dogs. Meanwhile, the big wolf attacked the calf corral, scared the crazy brutes so they burst through wire and picket fence and all, and scattered ; which gave the wolves the chance they sought to select and feast at leisure.

And one more crafty policy they had to baffle all reprisals ; that is, never come a second time to the same kill, never kill twice in the same locality.

Another trick was observed by a range rider who swears it happened just as he said. From a look-out butte, he was scanning the range with field-glasses, when on a distant flat he saw a wolf—a big one—lying dead. In the grass some fifty yards away, a smaller—a white one—watching. Sailing

12

above was a turkey buzzard, always keen-eyed for carrion. The buzzard sailed over, then around and lower, and deftly lighting near the carcass approached the head, for the eyes are easy meat. But in a flash, the corpse became alive, the buzzard was chopped, and the white wolf from the look-out came trotting to share the unusual feast.

But quite the most diabolical of the plots planned by this wolf team was triumphantly put over one evening after sundown. The wolver of the Anglebar Ranch had secured an immense female Great Dane, expressly trained to follow and fight female wolves. For oftentimes a male dog declines to pursue with deadly intent a female wolf, whereas the female Dane is even more hostile on account of the other's sex.

The white wolf had deliberately circled the corral, and left a mark of scorn on the saddle that lay by the gate. Then she howled the soft and high-pitched howl of the she-wolf. The wolver seized his gun, and at the same time unchained the furious Juno.

Away they went, the dog racing hard and mouthily baying. Away went the wolf at easy bounds, and silent, headed straight for the wolver's

set ; that is, four heavy traps around a beef head. She circled these adroitly, for her nose indicated the exact spot of each. But the blundering dane rushed in, and was caught in two ; then, as she thrashed around, the other two traps were sprung and she lay on the ground, perfectly helpless, and at the mercy of—what ? A huge grey wolf with reddish head, and a collar on his neck. She had no chance at all. It was chop, chop—and her screaming yell of terror was cut short. There, in the morning, the wolver found her carcass, and studied the tracks in the dust. A huge wolf, and with him a smaller one with mutilated feet, had been on the spot—therefore——

4

For ten years, this levy on the beef continued. Then all the cattlemen gathered for a wolf round-up. The Eatons, the Ferrises, the Myers, the Roosevelts, the Petersons, all of them with dogs galore, and horses enough ; and they swept the open valley of the Little Missouri, and killed not a few coyotes and one or two grey wolves.

But the Badlands were impassable to this invading

army. Here the riders were stopped, and their dogs that ventured in without support came back right soon—or never came at all.

The hunters did not see the great wolf ; but that very morning, the Eaton children on their way to school were startled to see, watching them from a near bank, the unmistakable head and the collared throat of Cody's wolf. He looked at them with mild curiosity—no sign or move of menace.

These boys were used to guns, and next day came prepared. But no sign of the wolf did they see, nor the next, nor for a week. Then the guns were left behind ; they were needed elsewhere. And the very next day, the wolf was on the bank again.

Whence got he such forewarning ? Where do the wild things get such supersensile information ? No one knows. The fiction of the Angel of the Wild Things has been invented to explain. Who knows ? This only is sure : they get the warnings if they heed them. And ever the great wolf kept his sense nerves keenly atune.

One fact came slowly to the knowledge of the cowmen now. The big wolf was alone ; the crafty white one had departed. No one knew when or how. The bounty, three times doubled for her head, was never claimed. They only knew she was gone. And this strange variant in the wolf's mode of life was seen : he still killed cows, but more often lambs ; and when he killed a lamb, he took it clean away.

5

Of all the weird fantastic uplands in the West, the Badlands are the strangest freaks that ever Nature upheaped in a mood that looks like madness, in frenzy of unmeasured power—castles, bogs, cathedrals, cloud-capped towers, rainbow-tinted rocks, hell-holes, sinks, endless caverns, death-traps, gas-holes, underground fires, glimpses of little fairy-lands, forbidding crags, infernos, and fairy dells, mixed, jangled, interspersed and fenced with incred-ible cliffs of treacherous deadly clay.

The scientist and the adventurous explorer per-haps, or the hunter, visits the Badlands as far in as he can go ; the cowboys rarely, for cattle cannot enter. The wolf hunter at times makes an arduous entry at least beyond their outmost confines.

Dalhousie the wolver was more than a wolver. He was a game sport. Nothing inspired him to

16

some wild attempt more than the assurance that it
had many times been tried, but never yet accomplished.   And when he learned that that thread of
smoke across the sunset gold came from some
strange subterranean fire that no one yet had seen
or even approached, he said : ' That settles it !   I'll
cook my coffee over that to-morrow noon.'

This was the immediate reason for his venture
into the fascinating beauties and horrors of the
' Land of Gehenna '.

He left his horse in a little gulch where the
fantasies in clay began.   Here was grass and water.
Then, with his grub-kit on his back, and his rifle
in his hand, he made for the place where the fire
was supposed to issue forth.   He wandered in
devious trails, and slid down dangerous banks ; but
ever he seemed cut off by impassable gulches from
the land of the mystery smoke.   Noon came and
passed, and still he struggled on.   It was indeed
near sunset when he realized that he was yet far from
his smoky goal.

In a quiet spot, he made a fire with sage-brush,
and cooked a much-needed meal.   Then, as he prepared to spend the night, his eye caught a moving
object in the next clay gulch.   A cautious approach,

2   17

a long study with his glasses, and he recognized the grey Cody wolf, hanging from his mouth a new-killed lamb.

The wolf was travelling, that is, going some-where, and knew just where it was he would go. He was carrying that lamb much as a she-wolf will carry home her kill. Yet this wolf was known to be a male ; and at this season, autumn, there are no young that need feeding in the den.

Dalhousie followed as far as he could, but soon lost sight of the travelling wolf. Noting the red-topped butte that marked the place, the wolver settled in his blankets for the night. Next morn-ing, he hurried back to his horse and made for home. The fact of the underground fire was interesting, but the fact that the much-sought Cody wolf had a den in the hills was vital.

To find that den was the big impelling motive in his thoughts, for surely this would end with a scalp on Dalhousie's saddle, and the ten times blood-gold in his bank.

This was why Dalhousie and his partner set out that day, with an unusual equipment for a hunt. Guns and grub—yes. Spades and picks—yes. But also a long pole with a wolf-trap tied on the end, and one small dog, a beagle of doubtful ancestry, and rejected from a blooded pack because he *would* run mute.

Fast travellers and keen hunters though they were, it was afternoon before they got to the foot of the red butte where Bud Dalhousie had seen the wolf the night before. Coming to the very spot, they encouraged the dog to take the trail : ' Hya—hya— Dummy, fetch her ! Fetch ! '

The scent was cold now, and not easily followed. Besides, the dog had no mastering desire to overtake the creature who evidently had left it. However, there was no grass on the place, and the clay dust between the scattering sage enabled the men to do some trailing.

Yes, there it was—the huge imprints of a wolf, the largest kind of wolf. The men tracked for half a mile, and then it seemed a new track had joined on, either another large wolf or else a second trail by the same wolf.

Now for the first time, Dummy the beagle seemed to take an interest. The scent was strong, and evidently this was what his master wished him to do. So he raced along the trail, loudly sniffing but giving no tongue ; so fast he went that the men were badly blown in following him. But they managed to keep him in sight, and after half an hour they came to one of those strange formations called sinks or volcanic blow-holes. At the edge, they were stopped, for it was fifty feet deep, somewhat funnel-shaped, and formed at the bottom by perpendicular walls of varying height. It held no vegetation except some scrubby willows in the centre, but numerous crannies and hollowed banks afforded shelter from sun and weather. In the centre was, as is common with the sinks, a drainage-pond, clearly at some seasons much larger ; but now, though down to the size of a blanket, it was the sufficient watering-place of sundry birds.

The big wolf's track led here. Evidently he leaped down into the sink. But the bank was sheer and six feet high, so the hunters circled round to seek out an easier entry.

They sought in vain, for at all other points the bank was higher and steeper. They were cautiously crawling around the farther side, when Dalhousie saw something that fairly made his hair stand up.

Here, threading his way through the hills by a different approach, was no less than a giant grey wolf, the very one he sought ; and held high in his powerful jaws as he trotted on was a half-grown sheep. The men crouched behind the nearest rocks.

With unerring sense of place, the wolf came straight to the sink, and to the very spot, the six-foot drop, whither they had tracked him before.

Arrived at the place, and without a moment's hesitation, the wolf leaped down ; then, placing the sheep on the ground, he gave one or two low whining calls.

In response, there issued from a near-by cave, not a brood of little wolves, not a joyous young mother wolf, but a worn-out, weak and crawling old wolf. They saw her happy tail wag as, with a growl, she seized the dead sheep. They saw the big wolf's greeting of the venerable old she-one. He licked her face, she licked his face, and he sat couchant by, while she, uttering the little happy growls that are part of a blood-feast, fell on the sheep, and feasted, and blood-licked, and feasted.

The giant wolf did not eat. Even the wild hunters were thrilled by the touching spectacle they had witnessed; but they were not here for sentiment, they were here to kill that wolf.

Both rifles were up in line. But from this point the wolf was partly screened by jutting rocks.

They waited, hoping he would move ; but he laid his head on his paws, and seemed content to lie and watch the old one's feast.

At length the men tried to crawl to a better spot for aiming. A pebble rolled and rattled into the sink. The big wolf sprang to his feet, looked this way and that, and made for the six-foot bank. Both rifles rang—bang ! bang !

But the wolf was racing, the men were hasty, the fire went wild. And with one mighty bound, the big wolf cleared the bank, out of the sink, and disappeared in the rugged hinterland.

The old she-wolf, sensing big trouble, though she could see nothing, dragged the rest of her feast away as she backed into the near-by cave.

6

' Well, we've got her ! ' exulted the wolvers ; ' and I guess we'll soon get him.'

And then they pieced together the various scraps of light they had on the strange situation. Here was the old white wolf, the old she-one ! Yes, there was the ball-hole through her left ear. Here she was, trapped in this sink-hole, the only way out the perpendicular leap far beyond her power. Here she had water and shelter—but what about food ? That was clear ; for in and about the cave were bones of sheep enough to prove that for a whole year she had been a prisoner here, and had been fed for all that time by her devoted companion.

To kill the old she-one would have been easy, or even to take her alive, for their plan had been to spread open the wolf-trap that was tied to the long pole, push it into the den, then the wolf would surely set foot in that and be easily dragged out.

But no ! The bigger, better plan was to use her as a decoy, and so ensnare her faithful follower. She could not get out of the sink in any case.

That was why Dalhousie and his pard set off as fast as they could for home, and returned without resting, with six huge wolf-traps whose jaws of steel were heavy enough to hold a lion in their grip.

They set this trap under the six-foot drop, the only place where the sink-hole might be entered. They rubbed their own feet as well as the traps with fresh sheep blood to kill the smell of iron. They buried the traps with the consummate art of their calling. They had brought a small ladder so they

23

could climb out at another place. And, as a finish, they swept the dust above the traps with fragments of the lamb skin.

There was no human trace ; there was no sign of traps, no smell of traps at the six-foot height above. The setting was perfect.

The hunters climbed the cliff elsewhere, removed the ladder, and hied them to their camp a mile away.

7

They knew it to be quite unlike the big wolf if he came back the very next night. Yet they must not lose a chance.

The hunters camped, and all day waited. At dusk, they came cautiously to a view-point. But the traps were untouched ; there was no sign of disturbance and no sign of the old she-wolf.

The second and third day passed. By this time, the old one in the cave was gnawing bones that once had been rejected.

On the third day, the men were casting about for helpful signs, when in a dry arroyo they found the perfectly fresh track of a very large wolf.

Without waiting for nightfall, as had been their

24

custom, they went swiftly and silently to the sink-hole. They found the big track again—and fresh. As they neared it, they heard the unmistakable clank of iron chains. The men rushed forward, and here in the grim and deadly clutch of at least three traps, was Shishoka, the big red Cody wolf—wrenching, writhing, champing the wicked iron with his bloody jaws, heaving with strength that might have wrecked a single trap. But he was held in three.

And, whining, wailing, cowering by, was the old white Wosca wolf, distraught, helpless, crazy to help, but helpless. She champed her blunted teeth on the trap that was lying out, empty but sprung. She ran aimlessly about, she chewed her own front paw, she grovelled in the dust and wailed to the skies.

The men rushed forward, guns in hand. The big wolf knew his foes. He strained, he raved, to get at them. The old wolf, too, despite her ancient fear of guns, howled defiance, and crowded up close to the big one who had loved her.

The rifles rang—and down they went together, riddled through, gripping the steel, gripping the dust, each with their last defiance. And two big animal souls—big, strong, heroic souls—had fled.

The men leaped down the bank, and stood beside the quivering bodies. They turned them over, they knew the marks that could identify—the pierced left ear, the missing toes. They knew the big red head and the brazen collar on the neck. They knew the records and the stories that they told.

' Gods ! What a wolf ! What a fight ! This is the old Cody wolf all right, and the one that he died for was—not his mate ! Oh, my God ! He died to save his helpless blind old mother.'

II

The Chillingham Bull

Many a time, my friends have asked for some thrilling story of danger from wild beasts—of the time when I was treed by wolves—nearly torn to pieces by grizzlies —or pursued for miles by a mountain lion.

My reply has been the same each time.

' There is no such danger. Wild animals, in America at least, let you alone, if you let them alone. I would undertake, if it were made worth while, to walk from Maine to California, and sleep in the woods alone every night, and never need a gun, so far as wild animals are concerned. A gun may be needed for my own species, but I have never yet been in serious danger from a native wild animal.'

This was my answer for long, but now I must change the story, and admit that I was once in peril of my life from a wild animal of a kind found in America. And this is how it came about:

IN 1913, while in England, I was invited with my family to visit Lord Tankerville at his home, Chillingham Castle, Northumberland, in the park of which are kept the famous wild cattle. These cattle are the sole remaining wild descendants of the uri of Caesar's time, when they were found in all the woods of northern Europe.

They still abounded in the Caledonian forest of northern Britain when Baron Muschamp, in 1220, built the wall of Cheviot-Lyng-Ham Park around the 3,000-acre range of a small wild herd ; and in the same place their descendants continue to this day, the sole survivors of the stock from which our common cattle are descended.

At first they must have been of several colours, dun or red with darker points ; but now, owing to centuries of artificial selection—deliberate elimination of all but the white ones—the white type with red ears is pretty well fixed as a standard.

The opportunity of studying this famous herd was most alluring ; and, accompanied by the head keeper, Lee, who carried a double-barrelled rifle, I was prowling through the park within an hour of my arrival.

28

In the middle of the wooded great enclosure is an open grassy space of about 400 acres. Across it runs a brook. This prairie is the wild herd's favourite range.

Keeping along the edge of the timber, I watched, and soon realized that I knew these animals very well ; for their every move and sound and habit was like that of the familiar cattle of the Western plains. In this, the month of May, therefore, I knew that the burly bulls with wrinkled fronts and massive necks were less to be feared than the alert, active cows ; for the latter had their calves at their sides, and were ever seeking for offence, and ready to do battle at the slightest hint of danger to their young.

The social order of the herd resembled that of the buffalo and other cattle beasts—the old grandmother leads. But the master of the herd is the king bull ; usually he is near the rear as they travel. The lesser bulls must keep away from him. Their place is on the flanks, and they must be ready to run out of his road.

There is one other prominent figure, and that is the dethroned monarch—he who once lorded it over all, until overcome by a stronger bull.

As with our buffalo, the average reign of each monarch is about three years ; and when defeated, he is not tolerated anywhere near the herd, but must wander afar, an outcast, quite alone.

One day I saw the solitary old fellow grazing a bowshot from the trees, and made a snapshot of him from the timber. Then, having picked out a convenient tree that would serve as a shelter if I had to run for it, I walked gently toward him. At one hundred feet I made a second picture. He raised his curly head and looked up curiously. As soon as he went on grazing, I walked softly nearer. At thirty feet I stopped. The bull raised his head, and gazed intently as I made my next snap. I could see neither fear nor anger in his expression, nothing but mild curiosity, but he was only thirty feet away and gazing. Then behind me I heard a soft whistle. I turned my head slowly, not daring to make a sudden move, and from the corner of my eye I saw the keeper motion me back. I backed very slowly, facing the bull. He stared until I was nearing the trees, then went on grazing.

' I wouldn't do that, sir ! You are taking big chances,' said the keeper.

The Chillingham Bull

'Yes,' I answered, 'but I got my picture.'

Next day, there was an air of battle on the herd. One of the young bulls was 'feeling his oats'—was beginning to dream of great joy and power to be won, actually believed that he was able now to take the king bull's place as sultan of the herd.

Bull etiquette is very exact for these occasions. The young bull began rumbling the heavy thunder growl of his kind ; then, marching with slow dignity forward ten paces, he began pawing the ground, sending the mud flying up in the air over his own back, rumbling as he did so, but suddenly stopping to raise his muzzle and pour out the trumpet note, *Mueh, Mu-eh, Mu-eh*, which is the challenge to a trial by combat.

The big bull neither turned his head nor stopped grazing.

So the little bull rumbled his thunder growl and marched up ten steps more to make another scrape and repeat his challenge. But the king bull kept on grazing.

Then the little bull walked up ten steps more— only twenty steps from the king now—and, at the exact right distance, made a new and elaborate

31

scrape. Then he got down on his knees, stuck his horns in the sods, and tossed them high in the air to shower down in black dirt on his own white hide, finishing with the challenge, *Mueh, Mu-eh, Mu-eh.*

Now for the first time the king bull ceased grazing, and raised his head. He did not look at the challenger, but steadfastly at a hill far away to the left. And the little bull picked out a hill far away at the right, and gazed at that.

They seemed unconscious of each other's presence as they stood for half a minute. Then who gave the signal I know not, or how, but they came together with a rush and a shock. The ground shivered when they struck, and the fight was on. Heads low to the very ground, snouts level and pointing backward, legs corded and braced, their great necks heaving and straining, and the mighty horns striking together with many a *chock-chock* as they fenced for the under-cut, while their heavy snorts told of animal rage and effort.

For a while they fenced, and neither seemed to score. Then the greater weight of the big bull began to tell. The young bull was pushed a little back. The big one knew then that he had him

32

going ; he put forth his strength, and the little bull was forced back faster. They came to a sloping bank ; on this the little bull lost his footing, and down he went. Then the big bull saw his chance—with all his might he drove his horns into the little bull, and gave him a fearful heave. I saw the loose flank of the little bull stretched over one horn. I saw him bowled over and over, as he went down the slope. And I thought I saw him ripped open, but just at the bottom he sprang to his feet and ran off, bawling, *Baa, Baa,* like a calf, and not torn open so far as I could tell.

That settled it. The king bull still ruled the herd, which, by the way, had gone on placidly grazing, and had taken not the slightest visible interest in the show-down.

Next day was the last of my visit. I said to the keeper : 'Now, Lee, I have three shots left in the camera. I want something good to-day.'

'All right, sir.' And we headed for the park.

There was some excitement on, for the cattle were all gathered together in the middle of the open part, bellowing and running around—' milling' as we say on the plains.

3   33

'There is something up,' I said. 'Let's go as close as we can, and you have that rifle ready.'

The keeper tapped the heavy express rifle, and gave a little laugh as we left the timber and went out in the open.

The cattle fled at our approach, but wheeled about, not far away, in two bands, one at each side, tails up, and heads up as they let off their wild snorts. And there, lying on the ground where they had been, was the young bull of yesterday.

'Ho, ho ! the big bull has settled him this time !' exclaimed the keeper.

Yes, clearly, the king bull had killed his rival. We went nearer to see more. And I must say I was amazed, for never before had I seen a bull in such a strange position ; on his back, all four legs up in the air, his head bent back, and jammed against his ribs, one long horn against his body, the other deep in the ground. How he got into such a fix no one could tell.

The herd ran around and snorted, with tails up and heads up, as I came closer. They looked very threatening, but I felt safe in the protection of that double-barrelled express rifle.

We went nearer, and were maybe forty yards

34

The Chillingham Bull

off when the 'dead' bull suddenly pawed wildly in the air with all four feet.

'Hello, he's not dead ; he's only " far-weltered ", if you know what that means,' I exclaimed, using the North Country word which means 'furrow-wallowing '.

'Aye, sir ; I know what that is,' said the keeper.

Now, it is well known that an animal so pinned on its back will die of suffocation—as the liver lies on the lungs—unless help comes. And the keeper said : 'Let's help him up.'

'Well,' I said, ' you may if you like, but *not for me.*'

'Why not ? ' said he.

' Because I know the first thing he will do when he gets up.'

'What ? '

'He will go right at you and kill you.'

'Oh, I am not afraid,' said the keeper, going forward.

'Well, have that gun good and ready ; you will need it.'

He laughed and went on.

'Hold on ! ' I said. 'This is getting interesting. I want a picture.' So I got my next snap.

35

Then Lee laid down his rifle by the bull, took the huge brute by the tail and gave a mighty heave. He was a strong young fellow, and was able to move the bull's hindquarters a foot or more. That was enough ; it turned the dead centre. The bull struggled violently, rolled over, staggered to his feet, wheeled—and rushed right at his rescuer.

He seized the rifle and tried to run, but I shouted : ' Shoot ! Shoot ! You cannot run ! '

But he thought he could, and set off across the grass with the bull behind him. They had not covered twenty-five feet before the bull caught him, and gave him a vicious toss.

The man rolled and tumbled, hanging on to the rifle. The bull rushed at him again, but the man, though lying on his back, jabbed savagely with his rifle, and the sharp steel muzzle-sight stung the brute's nose. He recoiled, but ran around, took the man behind, and hurled him twenty or thirty feet along the ground.

Lee fell flat, but hung on to the gun.

In vain I yelled : ' Shoot ! Shoot ! For God's sake, shoot ! He'll kill you ! '

He would not, and as the bull charged again,

36

the man, kicking upward, managed to land with
his sharp, hobnailed boot right in the bull's eye.
The brute tossed up his head, snorted, and swung
away.

Then, seeing me, he abandoned his first victim
and came charging at me. I was armed only
with a camera, but I knew that the worst thing I
could do would be to run.

The first thought was to get my coat off, for I
have seen the bull-fights, and with a mantilla there
might have been a chance. But no. I realized that
my best move was to hold perfectly still. That
brute trotted up to within ten feet of me, and
stopped. And we gazed fixedly at each other.
I knew that the next moment might be my last.
Still I froze, hoping indeed to hear that rifle speak.

It seemed a long, long time of silence ; then,
without any cause that I could guess, the bull
wheeled, went off at full gallop, and joined the
herd, which, as if in panic, turned and thundered
out of sight.

I went over to the prostrate keeper and said :
' Are you hurt ? '

' No, sir ; not much,' he gasped feebly.

' Why didn't you shoot ? '

37

' The—gun—wasn't—loaded,' he faltered, then added : ' I never believed they were dangerous.'

Yes, that fool had carried the gun each day because I insisted on it, but was too obstinate to put in the cartridges !

' Not dangerous ! ' I exclaimed. ' Well, now you know it. I tell you I know these animals better than you do, though I have not been here a week, and you have been here all your life. I know them because they are just the same as the old Texan wild cattle.'

I got him up on his feet ; and, although he said he was not hurt, he leaned heavily on me as we set out for the castle.

He leaned yet more heavily as we went ; then, after a hundred yards or so, he went down with a slump, totally collapsed.

I revived him, and again we set out for home. By slow stages we arrived ; he was put to bed, and the doctor sent for.

The medical man reported, ' No bones broken and no puncture in his skin ; but he's had a terrible shock.'

He certainly had ; and he was confined to bed for weeks. As a matter of fact, he never got over it. Though only thirty-five years of age, he had to be retired as a confirmed invalid. And all because he would not learn the wise and simple lesson : Be prepared and the danger will pass you by.

And that is as near as I ever came to losing my life to a wild animal, and it *was* of a kind found in America, though I had to go to England to find it.

III

Little Marie and the Wolves

HUELGOET FOREST is one of the great wild wooded stretches that cover the central ridge of Finisterre, that far west arm of France. Basking at its sunny edge is the hamlet of Carhaix; and here, on a tiny farm, lived Jean Trefranc with Lili his wife, and their only child, the winsome wee Marie, the idol of their hearts; six years of age at the time of the story, and gifted with every charm that ever came to bless a baby and its home.

Trefranc, like others of his kind, owned and thriftily farmed his three-acre holding. He had built the cottage with his own hands; a few hens and a pig were important in his scheme of things. The couple grew their own grapes and most of their table food; while firewood was to be had for the gathering in the near-by forest.

Jean had also some responsibility and some

revenue as woodman and semi-official game warden. Harvest-time, too, was an annual help ; then Jean and Lili both made extra wages at garnering in the neighbours' grain.

These many little interests, developed by their steady industrious habits, their good French thrift and sturdy common sense, insured for them a comfortable living, with promise for the years ahead ; and even a little *dot* already in the bank against the time when Marie should become a wife.

They were very happy in their simple lives, almost ideally so.

The forest, which began but a stone's-throw from their door, was wild and almost primitive. It was, moreover, abounding in wolves—not often seen indeed, but heard nearly every night. Yet, strange to tell, these nightly howling prowlers gave no anxiety to the peasant folk of Carhaix ; for it was said and often said and never once gainsaid, that no wolf was ever known to harm or try to harm a human being.

What ? How can this be ? What about the dreadful careers of Courtaud and La Bête ? Were these mere fables, or were they authentic wolf histories ?

There can be no doubt that they were true pictures of these terrible man-devouring monsters of the bygone time. There can be no doubt either that the wolves of Huelgoet are the very same, are indeed direct descendants of the wolves that one time scourged all France. They are not degenerate in any sense.

They are just as fierce, just as hungry as their dread forebears, but different in one great overmastering trait. These modern wolves have been educated, educated so that the fear of man, the terror of the man-smell, is over all, both the great and the growing. Never will a modern wolf face or fight a man. And the vast, compelling and instructive force is *gunpowder*, modern guns. By endless dire calamity, the wolves have learned it : a man with a club or a bow and arrow is one thing—a possible prey, never easy, but one that at times did serve ; but a man with a modern gun is wholly different. ' You wolves have not a chance against him. Then, shun the conflict that can end only in disaster for you.' Man-smell is terror-smell ; it is wrought into the character and training of every wolf cub as soon as he can run. It admits of no controversy. No modern

43

wolf will face a man or anything that smells of human kind.

This is the well-known creed of the wolf in every part of France—Pyrenees, Les Vosges, and on the great black broken forest ridge of Finisterre, in Huelgoet Forest itself.

The wolves are still abundant in that vast stretch of gloom. And it was from the famous wolf hunters of the region—St. Prix, de Keryfan, and the foresters of Carhaix—that we learned the strange history of Little Marie.

2

A small black lamb had recently been added to the Trefranc *ménage*. And, since the best and only free food was in an open glade of the forest, not far from the house, the lamb was tethered there every day under no guardianship but that of the gentle six-year-old girl. Yet the wolves that were all too plentiful around them were quite sure to respect the lamb as long as the human baby was near by.

Marie played about the door each day, or wandered off to pet the lamb. Sometimes she brought it titbits from the garden. And each evening near sunset, she went to the place, untied the lamb, and led it by its tethering-cord to the safety of the cowbarn.

There could be no doubt that the wolves had many times been drawn by the lamb-smell, and had crawled near or watched in hiding from some copse. But the presence of the child had acted as a scare, a guaranteed protection. Of that the parents were assured, even when the fresh tracks of some big prowling wolf were noted close at hand.

The wolves were rarely seen; but their signal howls at night, their footmarks, and occasionally the sad evidence that a sheep or a calf had furnished them a feast, kept the community well aware that the fierce menace of the forest was ever near. And still the family had no fear for their baby, nor for the lamb when the little one was near by to cast the sacred charm of human presence.

One evening in July, Mother Lili had as usual said: 'Now, Marie, it is time you brought the lamb to the fold.' The little one answered from a distant point, 'Yes, mamma,' and Mother went on to prepare the evening meal.

After half an hour, the meal was ready, but Marie had not returned. The mother went to the door and shouted : 'Marie ! Marie !' then set about other duties. There was no answer from Marie ; and, after some twenty minutes, Jean was sent to bring the little one.

He reached the place where the lamb had been tethered, but there was nothing to be seen of lamb or child.

Jean called again and again. Lili came, and they searched about, without success. Yes, they found tracks of Marie and of the lamb, and with them the tracks of one, or perhaps two, wolves. But there was no sign of violence, no clothing torn, no lamb's wool or splash of blood.

The terrified parents followed farther the dim trace. It led them ever deeper into the forest, and from time to time they sent far-ringing cries : 'Marie ! Marie !'

Soon the sun sank ; and twilight coming on, found them searching, vainly searching.

Jean was sent back to alarm the neighbours, to appeal to all for help in the search ; while Lili pushed on, and ever cried aloud : 'Marie ! Marie !'

46

Listening after one of her agonizing calls, she heard an answer—not from Marie, but from a wolf; the long, weird howl of the hunting wolf. She had heard it often before; but now it had a horrid sense of answer to her calls, a note of derision and mockery.

Jean returned with a band of the near neighbours, some of them woodmen and clever trackers. It was dark now, but they carried torches and lanterns. They had some trailing dogs with them, and these lent vital aid.

Half a mile away in the thick forest, the dogs led them to a spot where were the remains of the lamb—the wool, some blood, and some fragments of the large bones—but no sign of Marie.

Next morning at peep of day, the search was renewed. Only the best trailers were allowed on the ground, lest the tell-tale prints and signs be destroyed by unwise feet.

The ground was studied with minutest care from the tethering-place of the lamb to its death-bed. Kergoorlas, the second huntsman, it was who did the trailing and read the story:

Marie had gone to the lamb as usual near sundown; but, after loosing the tether, had fallen on a rough place so that the lamb was freed and ran off in a spirit of frolic. Marie had pursued ; and ever, as she nearly caught the trailing string, the lamb had bounded farther afield, going, as it chanced, more deeply into the forest each time. At last when, a quarter-mile on, Marie recovered hold of the string, and now was leading the lamb —but where ? She was utterly bewildered and lost, and so went not homewards, but farther into the forest which seemed to lure her on by promising openings just a little ahead.

Then the evening howlings of the wolves began —the wolves a-hunting meat. And maybe some of the howls had human tones, for they seemed to call her. And so she was lured farther on and away from home.

The wolves soon found the two wanderers, and prowled around and sniffed at them ; but, out of respect for the child, or fear of the human smell, forbore to touch the lamb.

Then wildly scrambling in the gloom home-ward, as no doubt she thought, the child fell down a bank. Yes, the tracks showed that. She lost her hold on the lamb's short leading-string, the lamb sprang to one side ; and in an instant was

48

seized by the wolves, apparently two, and quickly and wholly devoured.

There was the red record complete, but not another sign of the child. At this point, her last footmarks were lost on a gravel stretch that carried far into the forest. And, search as they might, even with the help of dogs, there was no further hint. The child might have been carried off through the sky for all that could be told.

' Carried off by the wolves,' was the obvious explanation. But, if so, why no blood or shred of cloth, or hint of human foot that any could detect ? And the older foresters maintained that the child was still alive ; that the wolves would never harm her. And, as every one knew, this little one, like all the peasant children, was accustomed to find the forest foods—nuts, berries, roots —and might sustain herself for many days.

All that day, and the next, and the next, and another week of days, was spent in arduous, patient, unremitting fruitless search. Then chill rains came, and washed out every possible trace, as well as wholly ended any hope that the child could survive under such a stress of cold and wet, combined with hunger. Yet they kept nightly fires burning on hills that might be beacons to the lost one. And every night, in every cottage near Huelgoet, a resin candle was set in the window, hoping it might help the wanderer home.

One by one the neighbours gave it up. They sadly shook their heads : ' Even if unharmed by wolves, she is surely dead through cold and hunger now.'

Jean and Lili did not give up. All day, each day, and ever farther, they carried their desperate search. And every night they prayed on bended knees to Him, who above all things loved the little ones, to save and send their baby back to them.

3

So a long hard month went by. All the country had been roused to the search ; and all the country —even the stricken mother now—bowed head in sad despair and said : ' God's will be done ! '

Two months went by. The sorrow of bereavement had settled on Lili's face. The neighbours had listed the sad disappearance of Marie among the bygone tragedies of the time, when strange tidings came from Treganteru, a place some thirty miles away on the other side of Huelgoet Forest.

Two charcoal burners were prospecting among the tall timber for a good place to cut the wood and make the charcoal pit, when, in a thicket, they caught a glimpse of a creature, the size of a dog, but covered with long yellow hair. The strange animal eluded all their attempts to approach, and ran sometimes on four feet and sometimes semi-erect on two. As they neared it in pursuit, it growled and screeched at them in savage menace.

The men believed in fairies and wild goblins, and were convinced that some such creature had fallen in their way. The superstition of the forest warned them not to spill its blood. They must catch it alive. And so, after an hour's running, dodging, and chasing through the thicket, they managed to throw themselves on it together, and pin it to the ground.

The creature screamed and bit savagely as they dragged it forth into the full sun. And now, to their amazement, the men found that they had captured *a little girl*. She was wholly naked but for the long flowing mane of yellow hair, matted with twigs and burrs, that covered her head and

51

shoulders. The rest of her body was burnt tan-brown.

A little girl she was in shape, but in all things else a savage beast of the woods, struggling, tearing, biting, growling at her captors. They forced her into a big charcoal basket, and bore her home to the village.

The news of the weird capture spread, as such news will. Men came riding from far camps to see the wild woman, the goblin girl of Huelgoet Wood.

Food was offered her, and water and raiment. She sullenly refused all, until alone; then went like a famished animal to food and drink.

The parish priest and the hunting nobles of the region came to see the Forest Elf; and news of the find reached far Carhaix.

In a moment, the mother's heart was astir and ablaze. As fast as horses and a chaise could carry them, they came, Lili and Jean. The news of their loss had long before reached Treganteru; and the coming of the bereaved parents made a profound stir, a fearsome mixture of hope and tragedy.

Without a challenge, the mother was ushered into the room where the wild girl was imprisoned.

The crowd was eager, hopeful, tense, friendly, and silent.

One glance, and Lili rushed forward. ' Marie ! Marie ! My lost Marie ! '

But the answer shocked her very soul. A savage growl, a menacing screech, as the wild thing eluded her ; and taking refuge in a far corner threatened with her voice, her teeth, and her blazing eyes.

' Oh, God ! ' came from the onlookers, as the horror of the change possessed them.

' Leave me ! Leave me alone with my baby ! ' implored the stricken mother. And there, alone, she kneeled on the floor, and prayed to God to send the true spirit of the child back into the wild thing glaring at her. Then, gently crooning, she drew nearer. And singing nursery songs, she crawled so close she could reach her trembling hand and stroke the matted yellow hair and the red-brown limbs. And as she stroked, the growling died away. And, when a little moaning was the only sound the wild thing made, the mother softly folded her arms around the child, and clutching it to her bosom, sobbed : ' Marie ! Marie, my darling ! My darling ! Don't you know your mother ? '

The wild thing trembled in her arms, the veil was rent, was torn aside, and the baby sobbed : ' Mamma, Mamma ! ' and buried her face in her mother's breast.

IV

The Wolf on the Running-board

SOME twenty years ago, I was staying for the winter with friends whose ranch was on the Mohave Desert. The great glorious basin formed by the crescent of the Bernardino Peaks was somewhat level and covered with a nearly continuous growth of creosote, cactus, mesquite, and greasewood, with here and there a few lordly giant yuccas known to some as Joshua trees.

We were on our way to town, the market town of Victorville ; and, in a good car, were following the windings of the trail that made with general directness for the settlement. Suddenly, we were surprised to see, about two hundred yards ahead of us, a big grey wolf.

At once the driver stepped on the gas in an effort to get a nearer view before the wolf should vanish in the thick and thorny brakes. But the wolf did not plunge into the thicket. He set off at a gallop straight down the middle of the trail, watching us over his shoulder, but galloping away.

The car had been running some twenty-five miles an hour, which is about top rate for a wolf on a spurt. So the car, going now at forty, overtook the wolf in less than half a mile. Still he would not quit the trail, but galloped and galloped a short car-length ahead.

My friend had to slow down now to avoid running on to the wolf. Why did he not leave the trail? There were openings enough in the chaparral and between the cactus, but no ! he galloped and galloped, ever watching us over his shoulder.

After a mile of this pace, the wolf began to show signs of distress. His tongue was hanging long and low, and dripping froth, his tail had lost its defiant upward perk, and his breathing was heavy and laboured, a succession of gasps. And still he would not quit the trail.

Another quarter-mile of this killing pace, and he could scarcely keep from going under the car. He was just ahead of the radiator, and his gasping was heard above the engine noise.

Then I said to the driver : ' This is not a square

deal at all. It is not fair to stack wheels and gasolene against flesh and blood, against legs and animal breath. Slow down!' So we slowed down to twenty. The gasping exhausted brute was barely able to keep from going under; still he kept to the trail.

I was utterly puzzled. Then to the driver I said : ' Can't you turn out a little, and pass him at one side ?'

This was not easy to do, for the trail was very narrow and had two deep-worn ruts. The desert brush was nearly touching the car. But, by selecting a flatter spot, the driver was able to get out of the ruts, and then run to the left.

The wolf dropped back on the right till opposite the car ; then, to my amazement, he gathered himself and with one great bound he landed on our running-board.

There he crouched, his legs spread forward and under him, as braced as the space would allow. His tongue hung out the side of his mouth nearly a foot long ; it was dripping with foam. He was gasping for breath and his heart was pounding his ribs. His head hung low, and his body was trembling.

57

As I bent over the side, I was close to him, his head was not two feet from mine. As I looked into his gleaming yellow eyes, I could see no sign of anger or of menace.

I talked to him. ' I'm not going to hurt you, Wolfie. I only wished to see you close at hand. I didn't mean to run you down.'

And, as I talked, the crouching head raised up a little higher. The slightly bristling mane sank down. Little by little he had regained his breath. His tongue grew shorter, and as we bowled along, the symptoms of a desperate run were lost.

His eyes were barely a foot from mine now, and I felt I was gazing into a brother soul. I wonder if he felt the same. I think it likely, for he was free and showed no fear and no wish to leave the car.

I was going to stroke his head. But my companion exclaimed : ' You are crazy ! He might take your hand off ! '

I refrained, though I think he was wrong, and I was right. But I talked to that wolf and tried to win his confidence. I think I did.

After twenty minutes, during which we ran

seven or eight miles, with the wolf aboard, we left the desert trail. Among the ranches now we were ; and, as we neared the first, the wolf looked hard at it, then hard at me ; leaped from the running-board, went straight to the ranch-house— and lay down on the door-mat. At home, yes, perfectly at home !

Then I remembered that at this ranch they had long kept a tame wolf, that is, a police dog crossed with wolf ; tame in most ways, but wolfish in his habits ; and in his looks not to be distinguished from a wolf. He had probably often before ridden on the running-board of a car.

V

The Wild Ways of Tame Beasts

THE WIG-WAG CODE

WHY does a dog wag his tail? Not by accident. It is part of an ancient signal code, a veritable wig-wag with a white flag. For we must remember, every dog that has any white on him at all, has a white tip to the tail; at the least, a few white hairs. For this and other reasons, we know that the wild ancestor of the dog also had a white tail tip. We know that that wild ancestor was a small yellowish animal with light spots over the eyes, that he was indeed a kind of jackal.

Suppose our wild dog-jackal sees a strange animal coming—a stranger is always an enemy in wild life—the first wise thing to do is hide and watch the stranger, that is, crouch in the grass. The stranger comes nearer, the crouching dog sees now that it is one of his own kind, therefore not desirable food, and maybe a friend. The stranger

is now so near that concealment is no long
possible, but it is very advantageous to impr
him, for that may turn war into peace. So
first wild dog rises as high as he can on all fou
and walks stiffly and guardedly forward, his iden
fication gland is opened, his odour is flung on
wind. Dog No. 2 also stands as high and loc
as big as possible; it is an armed neutrality. Th
are fairly well matched, neither makes a host
move. A moment's pause. Then No. 1, seei
no threats and desiring peace, raises his tail so
white flag it bears is above the level of his ba
and waves it from side to side. The other, r
desiring war, responds with the same wig-w
signal. The armistice is followed by an agre
peace, and now they are friends.

These things happened continually in the wi
long ago, and now you may see them every d
in our towns where there are roaming dogs.

ENEMY APPROACHING

FRIEND COMING

CAMOUFLAGE AND BADGES AMONG ANIMALS

When our soldiers were at the front in Fran
their uniforms were coloured and splashed
match the surroundings, so that on lying do

hey became invisible. But also each had his
national and regimental badges, and his identification disc for use when the right time came to show
it. These two ideas—uniforms to hide and marks
to identify—explain the colours of most wild
animals. And always their badges are on parts
of the body most easily seen by a distant stranger.
Thus the wild dog was all over of a yellowish,
streaky dead-grass colour ; that was his camou-
flage and concealed him when he crouched in the
grass. But his badges, the beads on the eyes, the
white lips, and the white tail tip could be held
up high at the right time and fully displayed.

But the identification disc, where and what is
that ? It is not like that of the soldier which is
an appeal to the eye. We must remember that
eyesight is man's best sense, but nose-sight is the
dog's main reliance. If his eyes say, ' Such is the
case,' he thinks, ' It is possible ' ; if his nose says,
' Yes, it is so,' then the dog is absolutely convinced.
Smelling is believing in dogdom. Yes, in all the
animal world below man. Man had a good nose
at one time, but obviously he had to give it up
when he came to live in towns and apartment
houses.

63

UNIFORM

The smell world is the big world for dogs and all the wild fourfoots. And smells and smell-power we must remember all the time in order to understand much of their action. Identifications that among men are made by the eyes, are among dogs made wholly by the nose.

On this big fact, nature has built up a great scheme of smell identification and smell communication, that is, smell badges and wireless smell telephones.

The Dog's Wireless Telephone

The important scent glands in the dog tribe are first the tail-gland on the upper side of the tail near the base, marked in most with a black spot. This tail-gland seems to be his identification disc. When a dog or wolf wishes to make himself known, yet keep neutral, the tail is raised at the base, with the tip or flag hanging down. The hairs around the gland are opened ; and the odour, no doubt stimulated by emotion, is allowed to escape freely. It is carefully examined and its aroma appraised by the dog who seeks fully to identify the stranger.

64

The next important scent-gland is the protometra
or third vesicular, deep inside the body, and so
placed that its product passes out with that of the
kidneys.

Just as surely as no two individuals are the same
to the eye, so no two animals' glands produce the
exact same smell ; it is the same in character but
varies with each individual. And not only that ;
but just as the condition and mood of the individual may be read more or less by the eye, so
also the gland oil varies with the condition of each
individual, and offers varied information to the
nose. So that a wolf discovering a stone or tree
tainted with the gland oil of another wolf can
tell at once whether that other wolf was a personal
friend or foe, a male or female, sick or well, hungry
or gorged, happy or hunted. The strength of the
record tells whether it was made recently, or days
ago, and the foot scent about shows whence the
other wolf came and whither he went.

In order that these remarkable news-stands be
of the utmost service, they should be regularly
established and well-known. Countless observa-
tions on the plains showed me that the whole
country inhabited by wolves is laid out in a system

of registration posts or smell-telephone centrals. Every mile or so is a high boulder, an old buffalo skull or a fence post that is the established place of record. Every wolf prowling for food, or merely travelling, goes to the ones that are near his line ; and by a brief study of the smell gets far more than you or I could get by seeing the creature that left them. He knows at once if a recent visit has been paid by another wolf, whether a personal friend or foe, a male or female, &c.— and if the previous wolf left smell of abundant food and came from the north, then the new-comer has gotten a very suggestive hint if he be hungry.

The behaviour of a wolf arriving at one of these smell-posts is precisely like that of a man coming to his club after an absence. He goes to the register, glances at the page, adds his own record, then makes a more elaborate study of those who came before, recognizes friends and acquaintances, and notes the time of arrival, &c.

So a wolf trotting over the plains arrives at a smell-post, makes a cursory examination, adds his own record (or if a female, leaves it on the ground near by), then makes a fuller investigation.

Friend or Foe?

Sometimes he finds the registration of an enemy, and shows it by growling and at the same time scratching fiercely with hind feet, while his back hair bristles. Sometimes he gets a hint of where to get a meal; and sometimes the record tells of a female in search of a mate, which at once fills him with emotion that sweeps all minor needs from the post of domination.

And our friend the dog! Do we not recognize every one of these emotions and motives in his daily life and habits? The attention that our city canines pay to the telegraph posts is the very same habit, only a little overdeveloped through idleness.

Rest assured of this, no creature has any habit through freak or accident. There is a reason, a good and ancient reason, back of every established practice.

Some Wild Ways Kept Up By Dogs

The wild dog usually slept where bedtime found him, his blanket was on his back. He selected a dry, sheltered spot. Then he smoothed the grass or moved the sticks and pebbles by turning round three times. And his town-bred cousin does the very same to-day, no matter if it be bulldog on the floor, mastiff in the yard, or pampered chow on silken cushion. Three times round they twist themselves when sleeptime comes, and down they flop. The wild dog had his bushy tail for final wrap, his nose and his four paws—his only thin-clad parts—were brought together and around them curled the woolly warming tail. And so do chow and mastiff yet, their tails may be needed or not, maybe too skimpy to count, but they keep the custom of their race ; and if the terrier does not hide his nose with his wig-wag flag, it is because the tail has been cut off.

Every habit has a long history and a reason. But there are two or three dog habits that have so far puzzled all naturalists.

Why does a dog bay at the moon ? Sometimes I wonder if he does. He certainly bays and howls on moonlight nights, but is it at the moon ? Wolves do the same. I sometimes think it is merely because this is a fine night for hunting, and the wolves or dogs are singing the stirring hunting-song of their people.

Why does a dog howl on hearing music ? Certainly not because he dislikes it, for he could go away. But he never does, rather he comes to join in ; and so far as we can tell, he is enjoying it and doing his best to be part of the concert.

Why—and this is the puzzle of puzzles—does a thoroughbred well-fed, well-kept dog, yea even a silken pampered chow on velvet cushions, in odour of sanctity, lose no chance to roll his body in the vilest rotten carrion he can find, preferring above all things the overwhelming, nauseating smell of putrid fish ?

Beating, trainings, counter-irritants, all are of no avail, there is nothing they love more to be anointed with than this unspeakable stench. If it is strong to us, what must it be to their exquisite noses ? It is like a wild spree, a dog bacchanal, the opium orgie of a ' Chink '. Their reactions must be, yes are, wholly different from ours, so different that some have called it the ' passion smell ' ; and a simulation of it made by bottling fishworms in the sun for a month till they have rotted and oozed into the last stage of nauseating decomposition is used with weird success as a lure to wolves and others of the nose-led tribes. The only known explanation of this madness is that in some way it plays on the overmastering instincts of sex.

Laws Observed by Animals

Evolution is now accepted as the process of creation. Everything we are and have is a product of growth and is still growing. If we look for the origin of civilization, we must go further back than humanity. The ten laws of Moses are supposed to outline our civilization. Four of these regulating man's behaviour to the Supreme Being cannot be traced into the world of the lower animals; but the six regulating man's duty to man have demonstrable application among the animals, for they are of older origin than humanity. These laws insist on obedience to authority, property rights, sanctity of marriage, sacredness of life and truth. The sixth is a summing up of the others.

Contact with man has always been ruinous to the morals of animals, and much good behaviour among the wild beasts is forgotten among the tame ones. But the law of property is very visibly maintained, and will serve as an illustration.

THE ANIMAL LAW OF PROPERTY

Animal property, outside of mates and young, may be divided into food, range and dens, with a number of subdivisions that concern the wild creature, but have lost interest for the tame one.

If you wish to gauge the property instinct of a dog, give him a big bone when he is not hungry. I have tried it many times—on one notable occasion at Petosky, Michigan, where there were five big Eskimo sledge dogs, really three-quarters wolf and showing all wild traits, yet tame enough to let me observe them. One of these dogs, the leader, was a big strong brute, a bully ; and one, much smaller, was careful to keep away from the big fellow. While the little one was alone near camp, I fed him a full meal and then gave him a big attractive bone on which were many good pickings. He did exactly as every wild thing of the dog world does. Without saying ' thank you ', he carried it off to hide for a rainy day, a hundred yards away in the swamp. He dug a hole, jammed the bone down into this ; then with his nose rooted the earth back over it, tamping it with his nose, but not with paws. Then he

71

raised his leg, and marked the spot with the by-product of his third vesicular. This was his property mark, his ownership sign. Every wild thing coming near would recognize it ; and most dogs, unless very hungry or very criminal, would respect it.

Presently the big dog, the bully, came drifting along ; his sagacious nose told him that there was food near by. He nosed this way and that, and moved ever nearer to the food cache of the little fellow, who watched nervously from a sheltered nook. The bully at last was within ten feet of the cache, evidently would soon find it, when up leaped the little fellow. In a few bounds he stood over the cache, his bristles up, his teeth showing. Ordinarily he was in mortal fear of that big fellow, but now he faced him and said as clearly as possible, ' This is my bone, I hid it, it has my mark ; only over my dead body will you rob me of it.'

And the big fellow—he stood up very high—growled very deeply, and scratched the dirt with his hind feet in a contemptuous way, then seemed to say with a snarl, ' Oh, who wants your old bone anyhow,' and slowly retreated to a distant tree where he put himself on protometric record, and disappeared.

Who could see or discuss this incident without noting that the property law was recognized not only by the little dog, but also by the bully ; and the conviction that he was right braced up that little dog to face and bluff off the other of whom ordinarily he was greatly afraid.

THE SHEEP IS A BARNYARD BIGHORN

Our domestic sheep is descended from a wild bighorn probably in Asia. Its coat was, as in all wild sheep, a coarse over-hair for hard wear, with fine under-wool for warmth. By breeding and selecting, man has made a sheep that has no over-hair, but an immense growth of the wool. Sometimes, in certain breeds of sheep, the over-hair reappears. These wild ancestral sheep roamed the level uplands, but they fled to the rocks for safety from wolves, &c. In these rocks was their cousin the goat. He lived there all the time.

When two males of the sheep battled in the mating-season, they backed up fifty or more feet apart on the level ground, then charged head on, so that it was a test of weight and strength ; and as a result the mighty horns and neck of the big-horn were evolved. When the goats fought, they had no space to back and charge. They met on some narrow ledge ; and, rearing, wrestling, horn to horn, sought to tumble each other into the abyss below. For this they developed their hooked horns and their marvellous ability to wrestle, pose and spin even on one foot. To this day the sheep and the goat keep up these ancient ways.

THE SOCIAL LAWS OF CATTLE

Our horned cattle are descended from the wild cattle that one time roamed the woods and plains of Europe. Though they varied in colour, the prevailing style probably was dun with dark face and legs, and white on the belly, also a white star on the forehead. Otherwise they resembled the long-horned cattle of the plains. The herd was led by an old cow, but bossed by a big bull. The cows hid their calves two or three days till strong enough to follow the mother. Their chief enemy was the wolf. When one of the herd was attacked, the rest rallied to the defence. When

74

one of them was seriously wounded, the herd turned on it and drove it out to perish. Such a cripple would be a bait for every dangerous beast of prey to follow the herd, and more lives would be sacrificed. Harsh it sounds, but society's first duty is to itself; that is, the first duty of the herd is the safety of the herd.

All of these things we see in the barnyard to-day. Nothing rouses the mother cow so furiously as a dog—the barnyard wolf. Nothing enrages the bull more than the smell of kindred blood.

The Cat Still Goes Its Own Wild Way

Of all our domestic animals, none has changed less than the cat. Its life is practically the same as that of its wild ancestor of the upper Nile, excepting in the question of morals. It is unfortunate that domestication has always meant moral degradation among animals.

Another common result of man's interference is the breaking up of the established colour of a species. The speckled, blotched, unsymmetric colour of domestic animals has no place in nature. Wild animals are coloured on a scheme which is

75

nearly symmetrical, and also matches the creature with its surroundings. Traces of the original colour in cats are commonly seen, and quite frequently a complete reversal to their primitive uniform ; which was yellowish grey with small, dark spots on the body, tiger lines on the face, and black bars on the tail.

Not long ago a friend said to me, ' In my woods is a wild cat, that is, a common cat run absolutely wild. She lives the life of a huntress and has her kittens in a hollow tree.'

Then I said, ' I will tell you what her colour is.' I described the primitive cat and he said my guess was absolutely right.

There is one singular habit of the cat that needs explanation. That is the eternal twisting of the tail tip. When the cat is crawling after a bird or watching for a mouse, it does seem as though success would turn on her absolute stillness.

Her colour blends her with the ground, her actions are perfectly timed, but that tail tip keeps on twisting in a way that one might think would surely betray her and block her every effort at a close approach.

But this is how it helps her. Crawling through

76

the grass is the sleek huntress, she takes advantage of every scrap of cover, her motions are timed to escape the victim's eye. She is hidden by her colour. Anything seeing her would see at best a furry something.

Another cat comes along attracted by the furry something or sees ahead the possible meal, and proceeds to stalk it. But long before near enough to spoil the first one's game, that waving tail tip, marked with the national colours of the cat, waves a signal, ' Keep off, I am a cat like yourself,' and thus the twisting tail invisible to the bird ahead, because the cat's body is between, is a wig-wag flag, a national colour that does useful identification work ; and the proof that it is so is in the fact that all cats do it all the time, and there is no other obvious purpose it can serve.

Why Horses Shy

It is commonly believed that our horses are descended from two different strains. One was the hairy rough-fetlocked roach-maned Asiatic horse of roan colour, that had ever to face and fight the wolves as its chief foes ; it was of a fighting stock and the males had huge canine teeth.

The other was a smooth-coated, smooth-footed, heavy-maned creature of surpassing speed, with dun coat, a dark strip down the spine and probably cross-bars on the forelegs, a native of Northern Africa or South-west Asia. Its dreaded foe was the lion, and its chief protection its speed. It shied at the slightest hint of a crouching hidden enemy.

To this day we see these two characters in our much-mixed horses. The swift one that shies and runs, and the slow one that faces and fights; for these were the ways of their ancestors long ago.

The thoroughbred racehorse is undeniably the swiftest creature that goes on legs. Its speed was its ancestor's great safety, and the one proper field for its exercise was the high, dry upland plains. For mechanical reasons, one big toe is swifter than four or five little toes on each foot, so the horse dropped most of the toes of his ancestors, and narrowed down to one toe for the sake of speed.

But—and there is always a penalty attached to such measures—he thereby lost the ability to travel on the soft or swampy ground and bogs with which the country was plentifully varied. His four-toed ancestors, like the pigs and horned cattle, were at home in these swamps ; but they were veritable death-traps for the one-toed horse. And to this day we see the joy of the cow and the terror of the horse on low soft ground. Unnumbered times have I seen it while driving cows and horses together over the western trails. There comes a fork on some shelving bank, one road goes low, the other high to meet again very soon. The horses, however old and trained, take the high dry trail and the cows the low wet one. There is no great difference and no danger, but both respond to the impulse planted in their race when their ancestors were roaming free in the wilds.

THE BIRDS, TOO, HAVE A PAST

If one were to leave the realm of beasts and enter that of birds, we should find a world of interesting wild habits persisting or occasionally dominating. Ducks, geese, turkeys, chickens, pigeons, guinea-fowl, all tell us unconsciously that they are wild things, suffering from the duress of barnyard life ; but they are ever ready to revert, to re-establish the habits and uniforms of their forgotten ancestors. Not a spot on the plumage, not a chirp in their voices, not a mannerism of leg or beak but has a story to tell of those other days.

Which one of us as a boy did not learn that it is hopeless to watch a stray-laying hen to find her nest, if she once sees you. It cannot be done, except by peeping from absolute concealment. A barnyard duck that is snow-white through man's interference will yet make his nest in dead grass and squat still as death on it, believing herself colour-concealed, exactly as her wild female ancestor did. The pigeon, descended from the wild rock-dove, will never nest in a tree, but only in such places as simulate the ledges and holes of its ancestral rocky cliffs.

Have you watched a pigeon dodging a hawk, and noted the sudden plunge down and turn nearly belly-up to baffle the swoop of the enemy ? Have you never seen a flock of young pigeons exercising with the old ones and learning this trick by example ? Then you will realize that man, by selecting those that did this wild trick best, has developed the tumbler pigeon.

The Wild Ways of Tame Beasts

THE WILDEST OF THE TAME ONES

But the most complex and interesting of all tame animals that have wild ways is the tall naked two-legged one that has long hair on its head, that has neither fighting teeth nor claws, and that lives in dens that are piled one on top of another.

Let me give you a family picture of this creature 100,000 years ago.

Soon after sunrise, the mother of a family came out of her cave high in the hills. At her breast she held a baby. Whining behind her were two others, a five-year-old and a ten-year-old; both of them were hungry and whimpering, 'Food, food.' From a ledge, one of them pulled down a rawhide, a skin of a wild horse killed by the man, and now used as a basket. On the edge of this the youngster began to chew. The mother took it from him, cuffed his ears and sent him off howling. The woman stared at the rawhide and at the three 'kids'. Her man had been gone for moons, maybe he was dead. There was no food in the cave, all of them were hungry. Game there was in abundance, but it was big and strong,

6

and kept beyond reach of club and spear. There were no wild fruits or birds' eggs at this season; but she could do as she and her kind had done millions of times before. She could feed on the bounty of Mother Sea.

She took the rawhide basket and said to her offspring, 'Follow me and put your feet where I put my feet,' then started down the rocky hill, naked, followed by her naked young ones.

Their cave was approached by a sort of rock stairway, that is a succession of rough footholds dangerous to climb at certain seasons, but desirable because it kept off many fierce creatures of the wilds.

At the bottom was a long stretch of tumbled stones and rock lumps fallen from the cliff. Across this was one well-known trail with easy steps from level rock to level rock. 'Set your feet as I do,' she enjoined them, and the youngsters toddled after, whining a little, 'Hungry, hungry,' but carefully setting their naked feet exactly in mother's tracks and in the middle of each stepping-stone. Huge wild creatures were in sight now, troops of shaggy horses on the distant plain, reindeer with branching horns, a family of woolly elephants breaking off branches in the spruce woods, and a big cave bear digging among the rocks. These were to be avoided without being greatly feared, for they did not bother the cave folk. But a couple of wolves whose grey coats showed on the outskirts of the woods were to be reckoned with. The woman selected a good club, so did the ten-year-old boy, while the five-year-old grasped a big stone. For a time they crouched and listened. Then she heard the wolf howl far away, so ventured on with club, basket and youngsters, and entered the great spruce forest belt that now lay across their path.

It was dense and gloomy, cut in all directions by the trails of the big game that abounded and that traversed the woods in single file behind a leader.

Follow-My-Leader : Keep the High Trail

' Follow me, set your feet where I set mine,' the mother repeated. As they entered the gloom, a big fallen trunk offered a good footing in the underbrush. Along this she led, and many a trunk was used in that same way. Not only is it good footing, an easy walk-way, but it guarantees that the traveller will not tumble into one of the hidden pitfalls that the cavemen often dug for the rhino and reindeer.

Soon the family took one of the game trails, the mother watching for warnings of pitfalls or of animal danger. And single file, a step apart, they travelled, winding in and out. Then the ten-year-old lingered to pluck a thorn from his foot, the trail wound round a big tree, he tried to make a short cut. His mother growled savagely and gave him a bat on the head. ' Go back and follow where I went,' so he followed the single-file trail. He did not know, and she did not express this thought born of experience : ' The woods are full of winding trails leading to death in various ways, or at least to getting lost. The child that does not follow exactly gets switched on to a fork that leads away, and is lost. For a child to be lost in these woods for a night, yes, for an hour or two, means certain death. Therefore, never let a tree come between. Keep the single file, set your feet where mother steps.'

84

Never Step on the Cracks

So at last the two miles of dark woods were passed, they were now on the open seashore. The tide was out, there was a great stretch of sea-worn boulders, slippery, yellow-brown with seaweed, and far beyond a long black reef lay bare. It was for this that the mother was headed with her hungry crew.

'Set your feet where I set mine,' she ordered as they began the dangerous trip; for a misstep might mean a broken limb, and in those days a broken limb meant death. No cripple had a chance; there were too many man-eating foes; only the very swiftest could survive.

She led them across the slippery sea-worn rocks, planting her feet always on the level crown and in the middle of the round rock. Then they came to a stretch of deep water in which was still the broken ice of the winter heaving and grinding with the tide. 'Set your feet as I do,' and she strode out with baby, basket and club, stepping carefully in the centre of the smaller cakes or at least never on the cracks, and the youngsters with amazing agility stepped nimbly after. They came at last to the great black reef. It was speckled with shell fish of several kinds, and in sundry pools were fish that could easily be clubbed—and then such a feast !

With bellies full and with rawhide basket full, they set about the return journey. The tide was rising. The grinding ice was yet more dangerous, but the long drilling was their safety. They set their feet in the middle of each cake of ice, avoiding all cracks. They trod on the high level boulder tops. They reached the black spruce forest. The sun was low now and the wolves were howling, and mother remembered how her eldest young one had failed to follow, had tried a short cut, had been lost, and had never been seen again. She said nothing but, ' Follow, set your feet where I do.' They passed the black forest. They reached their cliff and climbed to safety, to sleep, and eat again when hungry.

And thus on other days, and more and many more, she drilled into them the ancient lesson of the trail : Never step on a crack, never let a tree come between ; walk along fallen logs, keep in the cave after dark.

Here I have given you a purely imaginary chapter of ancestral wild life ; and yet it is unquestionably one that has happened millions of times, yes daily, to every child of the human race, during that long cave period, and all through the 100,000 years that it lasted.

THE PROOF OF IT ALL

What proof is there of this ? The proof is in ourselves. Watch two little children going home from school. See how invariably they walk along the top of a water-main lying by the pavement, how they love to balance along a low parapet wall. How world-wide and spontaneous is the old game ' follow-my-leader '. How careful they are not to let a post or tree in the passage come between them. No ! they form single file and go by on the same side. And how careful they are never to step on the cracks of the flagstones, always stepping on the centre of the stone, or at least away from the edge.

All children do these things. Why ? No one taught them. I never knew a child to teach another. In every case it comes from the inner impulse that was implanted there by ages of necessity in the days of the long ago. If this is not the true explanation, let someone give a better.

87

Why Do We Fear the Dark

There is one other chapter of the dreadful past that is written in our hearts and ancestral memories. Why do we love the fire ? Why do we fear the dark ?

In those far-back dreadful days man was the under-dog. The beasts were too strong for him. There can be no doubt that the human species was wiped out again and again in outlying districts by the wild beasts that were terribly fierce and strong and numerous.

We would not be here to-day but for the fact that in those early days our ancestors could climb a tree. There they sat in rows all night shivering and looking down at the shining eyes of the beasts below that were waiting for one to drop and furnish them a meal. Or if, perchance, our folk got into a cave, it was still a case of shivering all night with cold and fear.

The Coming of the Great Mystery

Then came a change, a stupendous change. *Man discovered fire.* How ? No doubt by accident, maybe in the track of a thunderstorm. Here was a strange apparition, a horrific, inexplicable thing that devoured wood, that shone in the dark, that drove away the fiercest brutes of the forests, that furnished a beacon from afar, that could destroy man—and yet that saved him from the beasts and warmed and comforted while it protected. This was surely the great mystery. And in order that it might not die or leave them, the wisest old one of the clan was appointed to save this blessed fearsome thing. The keeper of the great mystery, the first of the priesthood was he.

Now, thanks to this beneficent power, man was able to sit on the ground at night without being afraid. He was not engrossed with hunting, the darkness and the beasts indeed forbade all going forth, and now he could enjoy the society of his fellows. So speech and games and social usage began a mighty growth. Surely, this was the birth of civilization, and of religion too, for the fire was worshipped as the comforter, the protector, the great mystery ; until long later came the thought that that thing in the sky, the sun, did the very same but on a larger scale. There could not be two great mysteries—therefore, the one back of these two was The Great Mystery, the one great Over-power.

The burning bush of Moses, the altar fire of most early peoples, the vestal fires of Greece and Rome, the Persian Fire-worship, the altar candles of our own time, all are relics and proofs of this ancient story.

The Conquest of the Beast

And there is other evidence. When in some forest glade at night we light the camp-fire, the wonder-thing that turns gloom and horror of the woods into the blessed thing called 'home', do we not experience once again all the thrills and the fears and joys of the far-back time when the fire was all that held the beasts away? Oh, the horror of the word 'beast'—'animal' has it not, that is a harmless interesting nursery word : but ' *Beast* ' will help to bring it back, to make us feel again some of the gruesome fear, the appalling bloodchill that those things inspired.

Much of our superstition as well as our religion dates back to those dreadful far-off days.

And if, when walking alone by night in some

secluded place, you hear a step behind or think you see a shape in the gloom, a shining eye in the bushes or a faint low sound that makes your heart stand still and your hair sit up, it does not mean that you are a superstitious idiot, a fool or a coward. It means simply that that voice or foot-fall in the dark, those eyes or that shape in the gloom, have played on the chords of ancestral memory in you, and brought back with horrid power the sensations of those long-gone days when the eyes in the night or the footfall near, stood not for some imaginary terror, but for some powerful beast of prey following on your trail just behind you, and more than likely in a few heartbeats to spring on you, and bear you off his helpless prey.

VI

Padraic and the Last of the Irish Wolves

It was in the dark years 1650 to 1658 they roamed and ravaged in the North. And ye that would learn the horror of it must search the red annals of Tyrone. But for those who would know only the valour of it, I tell this story as it came to me.

I

IT was in the Ballinderry Valley that they ranged, the last two wolves of Northern Ireland. They were a giant pair that harassed every sheep range, took toll of every beef herd, from high Carntogher hills beyond Glenelly to Aughnacloy and west to Enniskillen, with Ballygawly lowlands in the centre, where the cattle were the finest and where most often were their raids.

A royal price was set upon their heads, as money

93

went those days. A pound was the wages of a labouring man for a long hard year. Two pounds was the high reward paid for the capture of a highwayman. And when a blood-price of three pounds was set on the head of Brennen O'Shagh, the famous outlaw of the bogs, it was a record gold, and speedily did encompass his destruction.

But for the two great wolves of Ballygawly, the price set was five pounds on each grim head —blood-gold enough to make a peasant easy all his life.

Yes, and many a gallant gentleman went forth to run them down ; and many a hound and noble horse was sacrificed, in vain. For the Ballygawly pair were as crafty as they were strong ; the dangerous host of hunters, hounds and horses could never find them ; and the farmers who sat up all night with pitchforks, matchlocks, bandogs, and bale-fires got never a glimpse of the grim destroyers. Only the unprotected herds were raided, and always the onset came when least looked for by the cowguards.

But Ballygawly was the favourite raiding. There had been no cattle killed there for a month. Two dog tracks, far too big for dogs, had been seen across the bog ; the long melodious howl of a

94

deep-voiced throat and far-off answer had been heard. And all the wise ones of the village looked about and grimly said : ' Now we may look out ; now make ready for a heavy toll on the Ballygawly herds.'

2

It was the good old Lord Fitzwilliam that sent for him, for Rory Carragh, the wolf-killer. One of the hated English aliens was Fitzwilliam, but he was better than his kind, and was ever ready to help his farmer folk. Twenty notches were on the shaft of Rory's spear, one each for a wolf that he had killed—he with the help of his great grim Irish dogs.

Many dogs he had lost in these desperate hazards, and more than one of his fellow hunters had fallen. But Rory, a young giant with muscles of steel and matchless grit, had never yet been downed. Rory Carragh was the hope of the raided valley ; and when Fitzwilliam brought him, this was the promise : ' Double the head money will I give if you can rid us of these pests— and all the help you need to do it.'

Then Rory's keen grey eyes looked keener, and his shapely lips came together as he answered: 'I want no rabble. I love the game. I will meet each single-handed.'

To the little inn in Ballygawly they brought him that winter night in 1658. Here the farmers were assembled, and the shepherds.

The potheen crushky was passing round while the farm group gazed awe-struck at the young athlete as he sat by the fire and quietly asked about the raidings, the loss, and the placement of the great stone folds, the sheep corrals, with which each farm was furnished.

The bog-juice in the noggins was flowing freely, and the tongues ran ever looser. Farmer Cavan told of his heavy loss a year before, a dozen beeves. And Sheepman Armagh, of his flock entirely wiped out. Then the gamekeeper, Foyle, he who had won some fame by capturing two fighting badgers with his naked hands, inspired by the red potheen, sat up with a savage word, and growled: 'I'd give the price of a drove o' sheep if I could but get my hands on them. I'd ask no spear nor club.'

And so they noisily vaunted and worked up a

wondrous urge for some heroic quest. But Carragh sat in silent observation. And a small boy in a corner sat in silence with eyes riveted on the doughty wolf-man, or timidly dropped if the wolf-man seemed to look his way.

Then in came Doolay Stark, the man of many sheep, that some indeed whispered was a Sassenach. Late he came with the latest news.

His sheep were all corralled in the high stone fold that he had built. No wolf could overleap that wall, and the gates were strong and tight. Yes, he had them well forfended. But, as he crossed the moor, he heard from the wooded hill behind the long smooth howl that never came from throat of dog. And his pony had pricked up and started and snorted and made such haste as brought them here an hour before the time.

A great silence fell on the roistering crew about the tables and the fire. All eyes were turned on Rory Carragh.

He had not touched the red potheen ; but now he drank a draught, his face flushed with the fighting flush, and he spake :

' This looks like a God-made chance for me. But there be two great wolves, and the two great

7   97

gates to the sheep corral. That means that I cannot win alone ; for whichever gate I guard will
be the one avoided by the wolves. Who now
will be my fellow in this game ? Who will guard
the lower while I take the upper gate ? And
there can be but one, for the wolves are keen of
sight and sense, and if a crowd should go, they
will never show at all. Who will come ? '

Now was grim silence on that room. Had the
priest come in and said, ' I want some gallant
lad to go to hell with me to-night,' there could
have been no blanker unresponse.

' Ho, Foyle,' said Rory, ' you that took the
badger in your naked hands, have you no hanker
for a wolf upon your spear ? '

' I am not well to-night,' said Foyle. ' And I
swore to my family by St. Bridget that I would
be home by curfew at the latest.'

Then Rory grinned, and sniffed a little sniff.

' If I must go alone, I forecast no success. If I
can find a gossoon brave enough, we both may
come back rich.'

Then a small and childish voice was heard :
' Would I do, Rory ? ' And Padraic O'Lachlan,
the fourteen-year-old son of Cantree O'Lachlan,

the lame shepherd, stood up. All eyes were on
him in amazement, and little murmurs broke the
hush, as Rory said : ' Sure, if ye have the grit
ye seem to have ; and I would your body was
as big as your sowle. But, for lack of a stouter
champion, I'll take ye as ye are. And if the raid
is on, we win.'

Then were the tongues unloosed. And some
were for hindering the boy's attempt. But Rory
scorned them, and pointing to his two great
wolfhounds, said : ' This is the forefront of our
fighting line.'

Mighty dogs they were, with the size and the
weight of a wolf, but not the jaws ; brave and
true as only dogs can be, ever ready to follow and
fight, not fearing the wolves when backed by
spears, as valiant as a wolf, but not gifted with
the jaws.

And they rose up with understanding looks and
deep-voiced whines as Rory rose, and girded on
his sheepskin coat, looked to his black dirk, his
skene-dhu in its sheath upon his leg, and poised
the spear that was notched with twenty nocks
significant.

And young Padraic rose like one who is inspired,

99

with quickening breath and blazing eye, he lined him up by the famous hunter, and filled out his chest with pride that he was allowed such a noble part in the train of the hero he worshipped.

Armed also with spear and dirk was he, and wrapped in a sheepskin mantle, for it was winter and the chill winds blew.

Young Padraic was guide as well, for he knew the fold ; he and his father had corralled their sheep there many times ; and off they went in the black night, while the roisterers at the house of the hill potheen—the crushky—gave them a send-off full of prayerful hints and commendation.

But when the gloom had swallowed up the gallant pair, the squabblers found relief in new libations of potheen, and something like forgetfulness.

It was nigh an hour before the hunters sensed the big black bulk that was the great corral, a thousand sheep within and the two strong gates, and the multitudinous sound of breathing and foot-rush with low bleats from the safely folded flock.

But not a sound of hostile foot, not a hint of raiding wolves, not even the keen-sensed dogs could discern a taint of any foeman on the wind.

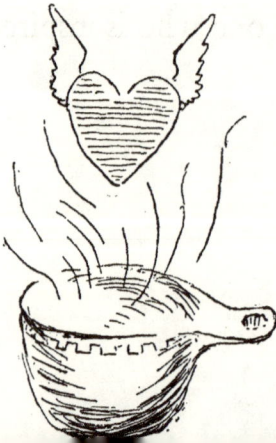

Then before they quite drew near, the wolver said : ' Now, lad of the stalwart soul, there be two gates. The wolves always attack from two sides of a great corral like this. It may be that the gates are strong enough to defy them. But that is not our game. We open each gate a little. I will defend the upper with my great dog Bran, and ye the lower with my greater Luath.

' The wolves' attack, if they come, will be between midnight and dawn. They will come one to each gate, if they follow their wont. And they come silent as shadows ; no cat could go more stealthily. Ye will not hear him come, but the dog will ; and, as the sheep-killer seeks to enter, will spring on him. The dog will give the wolf the first fall, and for a moment can hold him. But not for long. Now is your chance. Drive the spear through the throat of the wolf, and pin him to the ground. If not, he will surely break away, and rise and slay the dog and then slay you.

' And have a care as ye thrust in the gloom that ye spear the one right throat. It is for this that the dogs all wear the collar of shining brass ; even in the dark, ye can surely make your strike.

' Now, good gossoon, how feel ye ? ' said Rory. ' Does your courage fail ? Do ye wish to go back ? Or will ye stay and fight ? '

The hunter laid his hand on the child's shoulder. There was no tremor in the boyish frame. The hunter took the child's face in his two broad, strong hands, and peering at him through the gloom, he said : ' Well, have ye rued your choice ? '

He could not see, but he could sense the blaze of purpose in the boy's bright eye, and he must have sensed that less of hunter-lust was in his soul than of hero-worship.

Young Padraic had no words to tell it. All he said—and he had to gasp it forth—was : ' I will do—as ye tell me—I would follow you—to death.'

The big wolver stooped and kissed the young one's forehead, and led him to the gate ; opened it a little, and patted the boy's back, bade the big red brass-collared hound mount guard, then left them—silent, sturdy, losing in the gloom.

It was a murky and gruesome night. There were little whistles in the wind, and scratchings of dry leaves in the copse ; sometimes a passing scare among the sheep set them a-skurrying round the high corral. Padraic thrilled and started at each

small alarm, but he remembered Rory's warning :
' Watch the dog. He'll make no mistake.'

So, watching the hound at each suggestive
sound, the boy was reassured.

The dark hours passed, the chill grew deadly,
and the child was almost in a stupor grip of cold,
when, without other sound or warning, the great
dog gave a roar like a young lion, and sprang on
a dim grey form that loomed by the open gate.

In a moment, Padraic was all alert. Up he
sprang and poised the spear just as in the gloom
he saw the big brave dog throw down the big
brave wolf ; and, as they wrestled with ferocious
growls and strenuating limbs, he summoned all
his strength, and drove the strong spear through
the broad white throat which was writhing, jowl
and jaw, below the brazen collar of the hound.
For a moment, the great beast strove, and wrenching round he ground the hard spear in his teeth, and
grooved the steel. But the blow was true. The
great dog held him, and ere the raucous breathing
and horrid wrenching ceased, a shout was heard :

' Ho, Padraic, hold him ! Fear not. I come ! '
And up raced Rory with his great hound Bran,
and the head of the other wolf.

'Stavin gossoon! Brave boy! Your drive was true!' And Padraic, trembling with cold, and shaken with emotion, hid his face in the giant arms that Rory wound round him, and cried like a little child. In the stress of the fight, he was strong as a hero born; but, now the brunt was over, he wept as a child should weep.

3

Who can paint the picture of the pair arriving at the inn? Who can express the wild emotions of the hour as they burst into the inn-room, each laden with the head of a great grim wolf? With all that the death implied?

A vast sum it seemed, but Rory split it even with the boy. And those of Ballygawly folk who know the place and the story of the wolves, can point out to this day the very farm that Padraic O'Lachlan bought for his lame father with the wolf gold of that night—the farm on which old Lachlan and his children and his children's children lived and thrived, and ended all their days in peace.

VII

Rincon, or The Call in the Night

I

WE had two dogs on our ranch in the Bernardino foothills—Brander, a big brindled watchdog, with much of the colour and almost the size of a mastiff; and Rincon,[1] a police-dog of remarkable courage and sagacity. Though smaller than Brander and less of fighting breed, he had so much more character that he was the leader in all matters calling for a decision.

It is a well-known fact that at nightfall, all dogs, if they be free, revert to their primitive temper and pursuits—they become hunting animals just as were their forebears ere they were captured, tamed and house-drilled by man. It is further shown by observation that in these nightly prowlings, the dogs prefer to hunt in couples. Thus, it will be seen how easy and natural it was for Brander and

[1] Pronounce Reen-cone.

105

Rincon to go prowling and hunting nearly every night.

What they did in these nocturnal forays is almost unknown. We of the Bell-Cross Ranch suspected that the sheep and calves on the neighbouring ranches were not immune from their attacks ; for the night-hunting dog stops at nothing that promises food or sport. The fact that our own sheep and calves were safe, and indeed faithfully guarded by these dogs, proved nothing. All dogs respect and protect their owners' live stock—that is one of the best-known traits of the night-hunting dog.

Oftentimes in the evening, just in the early gloom, we heard the yapping chorus of coyotes on the ridge that lay east of the ranch-house. This weird cry always roused the dogs ; and off they would dash in the direction of the cry—or the challenge, maybe it was.

Of course, the coyotes do not stay to fight. They would have had no chance with the dogs ; and their yelping from the hill was merely a gesture of defiance, an attempt to lure the dogs into a futile chase, for one thing a coyote can do, that is, run. An ordinary dog has no chance in a speed match with a coyote.

The dogs nearly always responded to the coyote challenge, but usually returned in a few minutes to lie around the fire till the men had retired. Then, as if by appointment, both would rise and silently glide away in the night for a far nocturnal ramble.

Sometimes—not often—a different note came out of the darkness—a long, smooth howl, the deep call-note of the grey wolf. The dogs would respond to this, but rarely went forth to meet the challenge, if challenge it was. For every cattleman knows, and every dog knows, that no dog can face a full-grown grey wolf in single fight. Yes, even two dogs to one wolf is not an alluring prospect for the dogs. Dogs there have been who bravely went forth in answer to the challenge—but they never came back.

These were the ordinary happenings of life on the ranch. Summer and autumn passed with frequent repetitions of these ' conversations '.

2

Christmas came and went with its rudimentary festivities. The Snow Moon was waning. This

is the season when the wolves are mating. Trac
in the snow told stories of pursuit, coquetry, a
love-making. But the habit of wolves is to hi
away during daytime, so that we saw nothing
the animals themselves. Their changing calls, ho
ever, were undoubtedly signals—signals that
could but imperfectly understand.

Our dogs were more learned in such matters th
we were ; and variations in the wolf calls from t
hills produced different effects on our faithful tw

One night late in January, a long, smooth ho
came from the dark and distant hill. It was rat
high-pitched, and did not end in a gurgling ba
as it often does. Our dogs rose up quickly, witho
angry barks, but uttering little ' woof woof
They set out in the direction of the hill, travelli
quickly.

After half an hour of silence, there came ag
the smooth, high-pitched howl from the dark wo
outdoors. Again the dogs leaped up ; and wh
we opened the door, they rushed off towards t
hill, uttering the same little ' woof woofs '.

They returned in half an hour ; and, so far as
could tell, had had no meeting of any kind with t
wild thing that had called them.

108

Next day, I went to the place, and in the snow could read with fair accuracy some account of their doings the night before. A wolf, a small one, had been sitting alone on the hill. The dogs had come in response to the lonesome cry. There were signs of the dogs and the wolf gambolling together, but there was no sign of battle.

3

Nearly a week passed without any repetition of the incident. Then, on a calm moonlight night, as we were preparing to seek our beds, the soft musical call came faintly down the little hollow from the hill beyond.

Both dogs sprang to their feet, and out of the opened door in response. But now a strange thing took place. Within twenty feet of the door, and plainly visible in the moonlight on the snow, Rincon turned fiercely around on Brander ; and growling his war-cry, sprang on his long-time pal. Brander seemed surprised, but stood his ground, snarling. Then he tried to pass Rincon at one side, and go on towards the hill. But again the lesser dog sprang between ; and, snapping his teeth, gave the most peremptory and unmistakable order to Brander to ' go back '.

The soft, far moan of the wolf sounded. Again Brander tried to pass. The two dogs closed in fight.

Rincon went down, for Brander was much heavier. But being down did not mean he was licked or disarmed. He snapped with swift and wolfish snaps ; and Brander received so many gashes on his legs and flanks that he recoiled a little. Rincon sprang to his feet, ready to renew the fight. Brander did not retreat, but neither did he come on. And Rincon slowly withdrew and trotted off in the gloom toward the hill of the calling voice.

What time he came back, we did not know ; but in the morning he was home again, and apparently had agreed to a truce with Brander.

All day they behaved as usual. When night was dark on the hills, we heard no signal call, but the dogs heard something. Both went out together. And now the scene of the night before was re-enacted, but with less violence.

Rincon plainly intimated to the big dog that he was not wanted on this trip ; and if said big dog

Rincon and Brander—the Duel

valued a whole skin, he would stay back home and mind his own business.

Whatever his reasons, Brander decided to stay at home. And Rincon disappeared as before.

The next night, a wholly different scene was staged. At sundown, each of the dogs was given a large bone, the by-product of a soup-event. Brander fell upon his portion without delay, but Rincon seized his in his jaws and went straight off towards the hill of the calling voice. We could see him for a quarter of a mile as he crossed the open snow ; then, among the brush and in the coming gloom, he was lost to view.

During February, we heard no wolf howls, and but once or twice did Rincon go off with his ration. It was only when it took the form of a large and portable chunk that he carried it away. Often his meal was a pot of stew concocted of table scraps ; and these he disposed of at once, much as Brander did.

Then in late March a new chapter was opened. There had been several fierce blizzards, deep snow was on all the world. It was easy to follow and and read the tracks after a spell without the driving prairie wind ; and, following Rincon's track, we

found it led not to the hill across the draw, but to
a distant stretch of broken country with thickets
and a rocky canyon. Here the rising of the drifting
wind wiped out all trace.

We were unable to follow, but Brander intimated
his readiness to lead on. Yes, he did ; but he got
peremptory orders to *stop* from the smaller dog
who faced him as before, and plainly said in dog
talk, big and strong : ' You go home and mind your
own business, or I'll——'

And so the follow-up ended. We all went
home.

4

One morning, Brander came home from some
far midnight ramble, but alone. Rincon did not
turn up the next day, nor the next. On the fourth
day, he appeared, dragging slowly along, looking
like a wreck of his former self. His hind legs were
partly paralysed, his flanks gaunted, his eyes blood-
shot, his mouth gaping and slavering.

We rushed out when his return was announced,
and every one was ready with help or sympathy.
Our first impression was that he had been fighting

with an enemy over-strong. But we found no cuts or wounds on his trembling body.

Then some one said : ' He's been in a trap.' But his feet gave no supporting evidence.

An old hand who had killed many wolves said : ' Wal, boys, it's plain to me he's been poisoned. He's took a bait, but puked it before it was too late. He's been lyin' sick some place these last four days.'

As we all knew, it is the custom of ranchmen to put poison baits about all carcasses they find. These are meant for wolves, but there is nothing to keep dogs from taking them.

Yes, that was clearly the explanation. We brought the poor dog water. Oh, how he did drink !

Then we brought him a meal of boiled meat. He lapped some of the soup, but took little interest in the meat.

All day he lay in his kennel, moaning at times, and paying no heed to Brander's friendly invitations to romp.

Towards night, he seemed a little better. He drank some more soup, he ate a little scrap of meat. The trembling of his limbs seemed less. But he was still a very sick dog when the sun went down.

It must have been seven o'clock that night ju
as the gloaming was winning over the afterglo
when we heard from the distant hill the call that h
been so significant—the long, lonesome howl of
wolf. Brander growled and scratched the grour
with his hind feet.

Rincon suddenly came forth from his kenn
He was staggering, and in his mouth was a lump
something. I hurried out to see a strange scen
Brander was walking stiffly and with some sig
of menace towards the hill of the calling voic
Rincon was following with weak and falterir
steps, and carrying in his mouth the bone that h
been given him for supper. The soft wolf ho
was heard again. Brander rumbled in his chest, a
strode forward. But poor sick Rincon put for
all his strength into a staggering rush and head
off the big dog; then, dropping the bone, he fac
him with all the fighting menace he could conju
up. His legs were trembling under him, but I
spirit was uncowed. His mane was bristling, a
his glistening teeth went chop, chop, chop.

Brander could have downed him in an insta
but all my sympathies were roused for the bra
sick dog. I rushed out with a quirt, I cracked

114

once or twice over Brander's head, and yelled :
' You get back out of this ! ' He turned and slunk
back to his kennel. To make sure, I snapped the
chain on to his collar, and said : ' Now, you stay
there ! '

Meanwhile, poor sick Rincon picked up his
bone ; and, slowly crawling off, was lost in the
distant sage-brush.

My first impulse was to follow and learn the rest
of the mystery. But somehow, the thought seemed
dishonourable. There are some things in the life
of even a dog that we should have delicacy about
intruding upon. So I let him go ; but I put food
and water in his kennel against his return, and I saw
to it that Brander was securely tied.

5

What time he returned, we do not know, but
Rincon was in his kennel when I went out next
morning.

During that day, we did what we could for the
kind and valiant sick one ; and he made visible
progress. He was much stronger by night. But no
signal voice was heard. He lay quietly in his bed.

For a day or two, I kept Brander chained. Then, on the third night, the signal came from Rincon's wild pal ; and off he went with the supper that he should have kept for himself.

We were all of us much interested now in the friendship that had evidently sprung up between the dog and a wild wolf. The older hands, in discussing it, recalled one or two similar cases. And there grew among us a keen desire to get a sight of our Rincon's pal.

This resulted in a watch being set. But the wireless of the wild things must have spread the news, for never once did he come while any one watched. And even Brander, equally with Rincon, would do nothing to further our search.

6

The springtime dawned in its glory, and with it Rincon's strength came back. Nearly every night now he carried forth his ration ; sometimes in answer to a far soft howl, and sometimes without any signal that we could hear.

We came to have a certain respect for the compact that the dog had evidently entered into. We made no further attempt to spy on him. Once or twice, Brander, emboldened by our presence, attempted to take part in the proceedings, or even to go in response to the call. The effect was to turn Rincon into a fury; and, realizing that the little dog had at least the moral support of the men, Brander went back to the barn.

Many times that summer we heard the call. Then, in the long days of June, we could see that, when he carried the ration, our dog was headed not for the hill but for the rocky canyon whither we once had traced his steps.

Yes, it was in June on the longest day of the year that we got the light we had so vainly sought since winter. Rincon had carried off his allotted portion, a big shank bone of beef. He had disappeared in the scrubby land that marked the canyon opening. And we assumed that he would be back as usual in an hour or so.

He was. He came back—but not as usual.

One of the cowboys had climbed the windmill to oil the bearings. Suddenly he shouted out: 'Holy smoke! What's a-comin'!'

I hurried to the place, and gazed where he pointed.

' A whole pack of wolves ! ' he exclaimed.

Every man in hearing rushed to get horse or gun. I got my field-glasses, and climbed up on the ranch-house.

Yes, sure enough ! A pack of wolves coming. They were too grey and white to be coyotes, and one was much larger than the rest.

The whole lot of us were intensely excited, but we kept out of sight and stood ready with our guns. The man up the windmill kept softly announcing the movements of the pack, for he could see them when we could not.

The giant wolf was in the lead, and close behind was the pack. How many we could not tell. They swung out of the bushes into the open, and now we could see that there were but three following the big leader.

' Don't fire until I give the word ! ' I commanded. And each of us with gun a-cock crouched behind some hiding.

At a slow trot they came on, and they were within easy gunshot when it dawned on me—on all of us —that the giant leader was none other than our gallant Rincon. He was made to look gigantic by contrast with the others, for now we could see they were nothing but half-grown pups. Pups? Yes, the white beads above the eyes and the snowy breasts and the bushy tails all proclaimed it : they were wolf pups, wild wolf cubs. But, as they came nearer, the leaf-brown muzzles and ears, the black streak down each foreleg, the kindly relationship, all bore testimony that these were without a doubt the children of Rincon.

Our guns were grounded. We stood up in something like joyful amazement.

'Rincon ! Rincon ! Rincon ! Come on, good old dog !'

The cubs looked scared. They crouched and shivered. Rincon went to them, covering, protecting. By gentle approach, by friendly baiting, we got Rincon to lead them to his own kennel den, and slowly we set about a friendly understanding.

In the days that followed, they grew and prospered, and became a delight to the eye in their savage beauty.

But their wild wolf mother—where was she? We never saw her ; we never knew.

119

VIII

The Wolf and the Primal Law

YAN FYRO was a gentle scholarly young fellow of Danish descent. He was intensely sensitive, and had the most amazing sympathy with animals— not only sympathy, but knowledge of, and an understanding that amounted to telepathy. I have seen him walk gently up to a wild deer feeding out in the open, a deer that would have fled at speed from any one else.

Once at the zoo, the keeper was trying to force a leopard into the adjoining cage, and had a fierce battle on his hands. The leopard defied him, and the keeper's attempt was a failure. Yan was indignant at the brutality of the man ; then, when that official gave up the effort, Yan said : ' Let me show you how.'

He talked softly to the leopard for a minute, then took a tiny switch and said : ' Now open the cage.' The keeper refused until Yan said : ' It is at my own risk ; there is no danger.'

The keeper opened the bar-door, and Yan went in, softly crooning a little purring sound in which were often heard the words : ' Now, Pussy ; now, Pussy ! Fear not, we are friends ; we are friends.'

There is no reason to suppose that the leopard understood the words ; but he got the friendly emanations. His hair no longer bristled ; his growling ceased ; his eyes were not now glowing ; his long white whiskers like antennae took in the kind vibrations. The look of anger died away ; and gently talking, Yan reached out his wand and scratched the leopard on the head. Gradually, the spotted savage head went down, the creature leaned toward the boy, and a low, deep, catlike purring was heard. It grew louder ; and Yan continued making medicine with his song, and nearer came, till his hand could touch and stroke the leopard's head.

The fierce brute's surrender was complete. Yan led him gently to the other cage.

Thus would I sketch for you young Yan.

I took him on a long trip in the West. He carried no gun ; he had no desire to hunt or kill or

en trap. All he wished was to be with the wild
ings of the forest—to get in contact with them—
learn about their lives. Then something hap-
ned which no other man would have had the
ck to see.

We were on the Red Deer River, some thirty
iles from Calgary. He was coming into camp
e evening when he saw a wild skurrying; it
oked like coyotes racing. He stood quite still.
ey sped his way, and now he saw that it was two
yotes after a red fox. The fox was running for
 life, and was clearly much distressed. Yan
od stock-still, but began crooning his medicine
ng, a soft little wind-moan that expressed nothing
t gentleness, kindness, friendly emanations.

The coyotes were nearly on the fox, and soon
uld have caught and devoured him. But the
tle message on the wind went forth, the despair-
 fox sensed it, attuned his vibrants to its message,
de straight for Yan, and then dashed round
hind him. The coyotes now held back, and Yan
l hummed his magic song. The fox came crawl-
, trembling near. The coyotes squatted on their
unches fifty feet away. The cowering fox
wled up till he rubbed the legs of the singer;

123

and when at length Yan set out for the camp, the fox was following close behind. The coyotes, too, came on, but at ever greater distance ; then, when they saw the camp, they trotted to the nearest hill and disappeared. The fox remained a little while, then glided off in a different direction.

I mention these things to show the supersensitivity that Yan possessed when it was a matter of dealing with wild life. And it gives some notion of the Orphean spell that he had power to cast.

We had many little wild-life happenings in our journey through British Columbia, and he had opportunity to demonstrate his power. But the last adventure with the wolves was the one that meant the most to all who were privileged to see and sense its deep significance.

Our expedition had crossed British Columbia, coming out by the Fraser River, then up the coast to Jervis Inlet. The low forested belt along the tide-water is better held by wolves than was the rugged mountain land through which we had passed ; and now, instead of an occasional wolf howl, we heard them every night.

Following his bent, Yan would go forth late in the evening to some quiet place, usually a low hill in the woods, and there ' commune ' with wolves, as some of us expressed it. He had a wonderfully accurate memory for animal calls ; and soon he learned to distinguish the signal cries of male, female and young ; also the hunting cry, and the long moaning which was to the wolves the same thing as the song of a bird is to the bird—an expression of joy, of hilarity, not directed to any other wolf, although another wolf might make response.

It was a wonderful study in animalism and human psychology mixed when he began his medicine song to the wolves ; and always be it remembered he considered them not as menacent wild beasts, but as wild brothers.

He would sit on his woodland perch and whisper : ' Now we will find if that old she-wolf is about to-night.' And cupping his hands as a mega-phone, he would raise his face and pour out a soft, low, musical moan in a key which was fami-liar enough to him, although I could not have named it.

Getting no answer, he would change the pitch, lowering it a note or slurring it upward at the end. The answer would usually justify the method ; and, after one or two of these signals interchanged, a low, short howl begun with a gurgle announced that the wolf had come and was studying the wind not far away.

The idea of danger from wolves never entered his head. And when on these night expeditions I saw the gleam in his eye and the perfect sympathetic mood, I used to think : ' It must be true ; he was a wolf the last time he was on earth ; and ere he goes will leave us with better understanding of these wild things.'

We seldom saw the wolves. But one night, after one of these ' conversations ', we saw a dusky form come from the bushes, and slowly walk toward us.

Yan whispered : ' You stay here.' Then he rose, and uttering one or two low wolfish whines, he walked slowly toward the wolf. The beast stood still with head low, but tail raised at the base and drooping straight down for the rest of its length. Yan told me afterward that this was to release the musk of the tail-gland, for it is in this way they announce : ' Brother, I am so-and-so ; who are you ? '

Yan stood still, but continued to make medicine

with his mouth ; that is, mumble the little whines of a young wolf.

The stranger made no sound, but at length walked up to a white stone that was just ahead of him, and assuming a familiar attitude, splashed it with his kidney product ; then calmly, silently melted into the forest.

' He was leaving a friendly record. The kidney fluid is merely the medium for the signal musk. Alas, I cannot read it. Our senses are too dull since our folk quit the woods ; though every wolf in the woods can read it and know from whom it came. The woods are full of such stones.'

And his eyes had a greenish glint when he got back to the firelight.

A day or two after this, Yan went along the shore to study the tracks left in the mud that the outgoing tide had exposed. As he prowled cautiously along, he noticed at a point across the bay a curious bump on a rock. Then it seemed to move, so he crawled up and found it was a fine specimen of a hair-seal. It was sunning itself in the late sun, and scratching itself with its flippers.

Yan had not met the creature before, and was so intensely interested that he did not notice another,

a different animal approaching. On the same si
as the seal, but up higher and concealed by t
bushes, was a full-grown wolf. Evidently the w
was hunting the seal by scent, and crawled with c:
like stealth as he came to the bank just above t
unconscious seal.

Yan held his breath, and watched with eve
sense at strain. He bared his teeth and gather
for a spring as though he himself were the wolf

Closer—closer—twenty feet away—fifteen f
away—ten feet away—was the wolf from the 1
unwary seal, when, with a great spring, the w
flashed through the air, and before the seal cou
make a lurch, pinned him down to the ro
and tore his throat till his life gushed out brig
red.

The wolf stood over the victim, one paw on hi
and waited for a move. But surely—and he kne
—the quarry was quite dead.

Then did the wolf perform a curious ceremon
He sprayed the seal with kidney musk which w
his ' owner mark ', to notify all the world of w
that ' This is my kill '. Then, without devourir
a morsel of the flesh, he dragged the seal from t
wet rock up to a drier sandy place, carefully buri

he Lynching

the carcass in the sand, sticks and brush ; again he marked it with his ' owner mark ', and disappeared in the woods.

Yan came back to camp at a run. He was intensely excited by what he had seen. Together we returned with a canoe ; and, landing at the spot, we lifted the body of the seal from its hiding-place, dropped it into our canoe, and recrossed to Yan's outlook to watch.

' It seems a mean thing to do,' said Yan. ' It was his kill all right. By all the laws of the woods, it was his, fair and square. I'll give it back to him later. But I do wish to know what he is up to in leaving it there, and never eating a bite.'

For half an hour, we watched. Then, just about sundown, we heard the far-away moan of a wolf, then some yelps, that rapidly came nearer. The bushes parted, and out came the big wolf.

' Look ! Look ! There he is ! ' gasped Yan. ' But he's not alone.' A dozen wolves were with him.

He led them direct—proudly it seemed—to the very spot of his cache. But—but—the carcass was gone ! He looked all about, he scouted for a track

leading away. There was nothing. The oth
wolves hung back in a ring, whining impatient
a little. Then they also searched for a trail th
might lead away—that might explain the d
appearance of the feast.

There was no trail, for the tide had covered t
rock, had wiped out every trace of our landing ar
our interference.

Then, as the hopelessness of it dawned on hir
that big wolf began to look scared. He crouch
low, with his tail between his legs, his head he
low, his legs seemed sinking. The pack broke in
a clamour of short yelps and howls ; and, befo
we could realize it, the whole lot fell on him ar
tore him to pieces before our very eyes.

The meaning of it came on us with a flash. H
had invited them to a feast, had brought them tc
carcass which was not there. And, so far as proc
went, never had been there. They charged hi
with falsehood, and treachery, and they served (
him the sentence of the unwritten primal law. H
was innocent as he was valiant, but knew not ho
to explain.

As it dawned on Yan, he threw himself on t
ground in an agony of sorrow and remorse. 'C

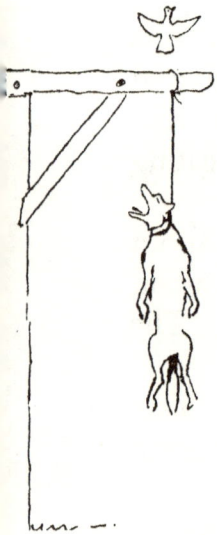

God ! I betrayed him ! I made him seem a liar and a fraud ! If I could only undo it ! Oh God, forgive me ! I assassinated one of spotless record ! I have murdered a brother of my blood ! '

IX

The Story of Carrots

THEY called him Carrots because of the coat of bristling red-h hair that covered his head, breast and belly e manzanita underbrush on the unforested foot-ls. When he became one of the Bender family, course his family name was Bender. And of s I am sure—if he had a middle name, that ddle name was 'Grit'.

An Airedale is supposed to be a hunter's dog, aving unto the man, and taking the babies as givable accidents. Carrots set all his affection on -year-old Si Bender the Third, and merely toler-d the tall dad who was Si Bender the Second.

Si Bender, primus and grandad, was a Forty-ier, and ultimately had crossed the last Great vide, in company with a fire-eating bad man io tried to jump his claim. His son Si had ierited the giant stature, the muscular strength, m courage and restless pioneering spirit of the rty-niner.

133

That was why he was up in the High Sierra, with his energetic wife, blue-blooded like himself, his six-year-old son, and the bristle-haired bundle of valour known as Carrots.

Si Bender's claim was on a trail that all signs said would some day be a high road to the tall-tree country. And the Bender plan was to clear enough land to furnish forage for horses, with vegetables, eggs, and milk for the house; meanwhile, to look out for the main chance, which was to take the form of a road-house.

There was plenty of game in the mountains, and Si-dad always had handy his trusty half-magazine rifle, so that with little travelling the family had as much venison as it needed.

All of which is secondary and of slight importance compared with the fact that the woods about the house abounded in squirrels and chipmunks of more than one type. These were big game for Si-kid, with his 'bownarra', and Carrots, with his speed and his diggers. By the hour these two would hunt the elusive and derisive golden chipmunks; and if the actual material reward was small and seldom, we must remember they were after, not meat, but sport, and that they had it in great, gladdening, soul-satisfying bumpers every sunny day.

They had established a sort of soul-mate bond so complete and sympathetic that by a few almost invisible nods and jerks, assisted by some almost inaudible whispers and grunts, they could get and give an amazing amount of information about the only important pursuit in life. Thus, by an energetic and repeated nod of his head, Si-kid could say :

' Carrots, there's a big fat chipmunk out there on a stump. He's chipping his war song to make fun of us.'

And Carrots, knowing the code without the help of a codebook, would rise up, cock the left ear two-thirds of an inch higher than the right, and give three brief wags to his very brief tail, which meant :

' Yes, I hear him, and as soon as we can sneak out of the house, we'll land him.'

The sneak-out was not always necessary ; but on certain occasions was absolutely essential. On the morning of my story, the political situation in the house made the sneak-out very vital. First, because the prospective battle-ground was in the

135

young garden where rioting was arbitrarily and tyrannically forbidden ; and, second, Si-kid was 'doing time' indoors, as a punishment for throwing a dead rat in the spring hole.

But the sinister plans of the shameless two succeeded so far that they got away unseen by Mother, and Father was off chopping in the field that was to be.

Carrots' senses were of the most exquisite accuracy ; and when the two accomplices had reassembled in the forbidden garden, there, indeed, was the chipmunk, on a root, uttering his staccato 'Chip, chip, chip', but the overtone of the music was an insistent 'Jacob, Jacob' from a dozen woodpeckers that were assailing something in a distant tree.

The woodpeckers' cries are far-flung notice of some creature at bay, and the red-headed dog and the tow-topped boy raced for the spot. There was not much to see when they got there. A number of woodpeckers skimming and racketing about a thick place away up in a young pine tree. The thick place looked interesting, but kept its secret until, mounted on a near stump, Si-kid caught a glimpse of a long black-and-white-ringed tail. He had seen a tail like that before. Si-dad once brought in a creature that wore one, and called it a coon cat or ringtail of the woods.

A bow with blunt arrows is good medicine for chipmunks, squirrels, and birds ; but a ringtail is big game. Valiantly and vainly did Si-kid shoot again and again, to see each and every arrow bound off some heavy limb, but leave the ringtail unharmed. Carrots yelled uproarious applause, and threatened to climb the tree unless the ringtail came down at once ; and, to prove that he meant it, rushed up the trunk for a distance of three or four feet, and many times.

Si-kid had never been to Sunday-school, so that his language was rude, rough, and too strong to be printed here. He had learned it chiefly from his dad. And though Mother said sometimes, ' See here, now, kid, that word's too big for a mouth your size,' there was no sense in forbidding him to copy the only model in sight.

Therefore, I shall not tell you what he said about that ringtail and things in general. It did not make much difference, anyway, for the only two who heard were the ringtail, who did not understand, and the dog, who cordially approved.

137

This riot had continued without the least symptom of success when Carrots, who had a practical streak as well as the unbounded enthusiasm of a fanatic, sat off to one side, watched Si-kid shoot three times more with his blunt arrow, gave a low woof, which meant, ' Say, kid ' ; cocked his head on one side, which was the high sign for ' Got an idea ' ; then looked longingly toward the cabin. Si-kid paused as he prepared to shoot again, Carrots gave another woof, and started for the cabin.

' Woof, woof,' he said. Si-kid made some shocking remarks, shot his bolt again, then, impressed by the persistency of his colleague, went to see what it meant. His first thought was that Si-dad was coming with swift retribution for sundry breaches of law and order. But, no, Dad was still afar at the chopping, and when the dog scratched at the cabin door Mother was nowhere in sight.

Little Si opened the door, and then Carrots showed his hand—he reared up against the wall under the rifle hanging from a pair of deer horns, and gave an unmistakably comprehending ' Woof, woof, woof ', telling Si-kid just as plainly as print that ' bowsenarras ' are all right for small game, but big game needs the rifle.

138

It had hung there day and night, as far back as Si-kid could remember, except when Dad took it to get meat ; and in the magazine, so he had heard, were just six cartridges, no more, no less, for Si-dad used to say :

' A man who couldn't get all the meat he needed in six shots oughter go hungry.'

Si-kid had been sternly forbidden to touch the precious rifle, and knew perfectly well the letter of the law. But we know, and he felt without knowing, that great emergencies must override all technicalities of the law. There is a code for peace, and another for war. Here was an emergency of the greatest magnitude, and Carrots had voted for extreme measures. The kid peered around for signs of his rulers. They were nowhere to be seen. The woodpeckers had redoubled their outcries, proving that the game was astir, probably escaping. That settled it. He moved his own high chair to the wall under the rifle, carefully climbed, lifted the weapon from its antler hooks, got down, made for the door, and hurried out to bump into his mother.

' Hyar, you darned kid, where you going with that gun ? '

She seized the rifle and aimed a cuff at his head,

which he dodged with the adroitness born of much experience. Si fled to a safe distance, Carrots looked puzzled. Then Si began :

' Well, there's a big ringtail out in the woods, an' I wanted to git him.'

' You let that gun alone ; hain't I tole you before ? Ten years from now is time enough for you to handle a rifle.'

So the kid and the pup went off defeated, to shout and objurgate the ringtail, and wish Dad was home.

Mother took the rifle in ; then reflecting, ' Never can tell what he'll do,' she took out the six cartridges, and set them in a row on a high safe shelf, where Dad would surely see them if needed ; hung up the empty rifle, and went off with her pail to pick a mess of huckleberries for dinner.

Si-dad was chopping away steadily ; but once, as he stopped for a spell, his keen grey eye caught sight of something running in the near woods, a furry coat, a flash of white. With true hunter instinct, he froze for a moment, then got a glimpse of antlers. That was enough. With long, silent strides he made for the cabin, seized the trusty rifle, and went out for meat.

The buck had disappeared, but the trail was plain,

and he followed it, a stealthy follow for a quarter-mile. Again he glimpsed the white flag, but the deer was behind a tree. He was manœuvring to a better view, not forgetting the wind, when a pine squirrel espied the hunter and began such a tirade that the game took the hint and, without actually bounding, moved briskly away.

Si Bender followed quickly, and he had a momentary view of a fine big fat buck, a real prize. Now he followed eagerly. The tracks showed a steady walk, hardly flight, and Si knew that in a certain open glade, just ahead, he would surely sight the buck. Then one short sharp whistle would turn it into a statue, and one short sharp shot would turn it into meat.

So he followed. But just this side of the opening he found the signs of frantic bounding ; great hoof-made furrows, long spaces from track to track, and signs of escaping that were puzzling till Si read in the trail the other signs—the tracks of a mountain lion—proofs that from ambush he had sprung at the deer and missed.

At first this seemed to end all hope of a successful chase, till Si remembered that he might get a lion skin instead.

Now he followed carefully. The bounding had continued, but he saw no sign of the pursuer. The deer, evidently but a little scared and quite unhurt, had gone fast for a mile, then settled down to a walk. Now, strange to say—the track told it— the buck had turned on a little knoll, and looked back as though searching curiously for his foe. That was promising, and Si went trailing swiftly, but with great caution, listening intently from time to time. Si went another mile, till he heard the pine squirrels scolding, and the mountain jays wailing, in a fashion that generally means, 'There's something doing.'

Then in a muddy place, he found plainly the trail of the buck, and, following it, the tracks of not one but two mountain lions, a big one and a smaller one, undoubtedly a pair. So far there was no alarm written in the buck's track, which only increased its danger.

Out of the pine woods, the storyful trail led on. The jays and pine squirrels grew silent for a space, which might mean only that the country was more open, though harder, for manzanita and buckbrush now spread their barbed wires over broken rock and little breadths of sloping hill. Si quit the track for an easy road around, then, rising to a shoulder of the hill, got a flying view of the deer as it lightly leaped down and out of sight. Then, too, he caught a flash of brown—a long-tailed beast, which disappeared at the same place as the deer, and the outcry of the jays was redoubled.

Now was the chance of all the chase. The lion had surely downed the deer, and skilfully Si Bender made his silent way to the edge. It was a drop of nearly ten feet sheer into a ravine whose lower end was lost in a few low trees, and no living thing in sight. Si swung softly to the bottom, and then, in a flash, he saw what he had sought—the deer laid low, and, clutching its quivering form, lapping the hot blood, not one, but two, a pair of mountain lions only thirty yards away.

They saw him at the same moment, all their wild ferocity aroused by the blood-lust, their hunger, and their sense of ownership. With ears laid back and wrinkled snarling faces, they turned his way. Calmly he cocked his gun, and, moving a little aside and forward for a clearer view, he seemed to challenge them. And they, proud and fearless in their conscious power, accepted the challenge, and stalked high and menacing toward him. The

trusty rifle was levelled between the eyes of th
bigger. There was never a shake of that stron;
hand as he gave the death-dealing tug to the trigger
The hammer struck with an idle click.

What ! The gun-chamber empty and the lion
closing in ! Si jerked the lever to throw in
second cartridge. Again the hammer clicked. H
jerked the lever again, and again in vain ; and nov
he knew that he had an empty gun, and was coope
in at the mercy of two bloodthirsty lions, agains
either one of which he stood no shadow of a chanc(
He loosed his knife, and clutched the empty gun fc
a club, feeling indeed that he had to die, but woul
not die alone.

The lions separated, but closed in on either side
one at least would attack from behind. But S
backed up to the relentless wall and seized the gui
and yelled in hope that the human voice might hel
to hold them back. The only answer for a momer
was the rumbling growls of the certain deat
approaching. Then the bluejays screamed, and th
wood was filled with mighty yelping of a pac
of hounds, and racing madly into the little gulc
of death came a yelling, bounding, red-headed dog
' Yap, yap, yap,' like a mad thing he dashed

the lions, as though they were but chipmunks ; and the lions, though bold and ferocious brutes, are sometimes strangely upset by such a sudden uproar as the fury of a raging, yelping dog.

They recoiled, and, not for fear, but for better observation, each lightly sprang up into a low tree, while Carrots, fearless, reckless little Carrots, raced near and yelled, cutting figures of eight around the two trees, and daring them by all the powers of death and destruction to come down and be torn to pieces by his small fearless jaws.

For a moment it seemed but a trifling respite. It had sounded like a yelling pack, but now it was only one red cur.   In a second, the monsters would leap down and tear him open with a blow, then end the hunter.   But Carrots, crazy as a loon, was also wise.   He dashed in greeting to the doomed hunter, leaped on him, and, lo, hanging to the puppy's hairy neck the hunter saw a little bag.   He gripped it in a tremor of amazement, knife-ripped it open. *It held the six missing cartridges.*   He quickly forced them into the gun.

' *Bang, bang,*' and heavily thudding on the ground fell the two great, grim, tawny brutes, to gurgle out their lives as they clutched the earth and furrowed a near log with their mighty claws—then to shiver and lie still.

Carrots shouted for joy, and tugged valiantly at the sodden, immovable carcasses of the foe, then sat on a distant log, while Si took the quarters of the buck, and homeward they marched. Shall I tell it ? As they left that gulch, there came over that big, strong man a sudden weakness, his hands and his knees trembled, his eyes grew dim. Then Carrots came and shoved his bristling nose into the man's hand, and said some things in Airedale that Si-dad did not know, but Si-kid could have turned into good mountain English.

The weakness, the surge-reaction passed. Si-dad set out for home. The bluejays screamed, and the red squirrels chippered as he passed. Carrots walked near for a while, then, seeming to say, ' You don't need me any more,' trotted off to the cabin, where his empty neck-bag told a happy tale.

It looked like a miracle, the work of an angel with knowledge and power ; but Si-dad had partly guessed it before he got home. His wife had found the rifle gone and the six cartridges still on the shelf. Alas ! her man had gone with an empty gun, and did not know it. Then came the happy thought to

146

send them by a messenger, the only one who could quickly and surely follow the trail, and Carrots came —not one small second oversoon.

There were tears in the woman's brave eyes when she heard it all, tears of joy and terror and gratitude.

But all their efforts to make a hero of Carrots were failures. He simply looked bored, and told them as plainly as he could in good, strong Airedale :

' Oh, forget it. I didn't do it for you. I only did it so you wouldn't lick the kid for stealing the gun.'

X

Chicaree

An Adventure in the Life of a Red Squirrel

'SNICK, *Snick, Snick, Snicker,*' he called again and again, from the safe top of a poplar tree. That was his challenge and his derision of a dog that had chased him that day, for the hundredth time. The dog glared at the tree; but, disdaining to give even one bark in reply, went off and lay down.

Chicaree was by no means at home in the poplar. It stood by itself in the pasture; it had no nuts to offer; but it was a convenient half-way harbour on such times when he ventured to raid the chicken yard for a share of corn. He was up the tree now because his inveterate enemy had forced him there. He hurled his defiance more than once, but he was well satisfied to have the dog ignore him, in view of the perilous overland trip he must make before he could reach his home woods.

Now for a long spell, he lay silently watching.

149

The dog still slept. Then Chicaree slipped quietly down the far side of the tree, and skurried across the pasture.

He had not gone half-way, when he made a wonderful find—a rare red mushroom, a russula.

The red russula is something more than food—it is a delicacy and a delightful stimulant. Its luscious peppery pulp is to the red squirrel much the same as brandied peaches to human beings, highly acceptable to all—a passion to some.

Chicaree loved the red russula inordinately. He could no more go by that fine big rose-top than an old toper could go by a free drink of his favourite brew. With a wrench of his paws, he broke it loose at the root ; holding the stem in his teeth, he bounded on to his home woods. But the broad umbrella of the mushroom blocked his view, and he bumped with full force into a root that did him no harm indeed, but it shattered his prize to bits.

Oh, how mad he was ! He sputtered and scolded at that root, as though it were an active, wilful enemy. His great red tail, held low as he travelled, was now high in the air over his head, and jerked about as he chattered. A bad combina-

tion for him ; for the noise awakened the dog, and the tail showed plainly whence it came. The enemy was within twenty-five hops before the irate little epicure realized his peril, and set off at his best pace ; while the dog followed with whoops of delight at every jump, for now surely his turn had come.

In a straightaway race, the squirrel would have stood no chance at all. None knew that better than himself. Not half of the distance to the friendly trees was covered, before the dog overtook him. But Chicaree had training for just such an attack. He sprang sidewise and a little backward, with all his force, and the dog's white teeth snapped harmlessly in the air. Then began a most extraordinary baffling series of zigzag bounds. This way, that, back and forth, but ever nearing, not the woods, but a low mound a score of jumps away. Chicaree was straining all his powers to get there. The dog had no plan, except to seize and crush his bright little foe. What possible protection could Chicaree find in a low mound ? He knew ; in one heart-beat more he was there. He was at a woodchuck's mound and by it of course the woodchuck's den. Like a flash he went down, and was safe. And the huge brute that was trying so hard to destroy him, rammed his ugly head down the burrow as far as he could reach. He tore with claws and teeth to enlarge it, and made horrid mouthings at the door. And Chicaree ! What was he doing ? Shivering with fear ? Not at all, he knew this game. He knew quite well the plan of the den.

Every woodchuck makes his house with two entrances—one, the first made, is that from which most of the earth is scratched. It is little used afterwards, sometimes it closes up, and usually, it has a growth of tall weeds about it.

Now this back door was Chicaree's salvation. Far underground was the den, long abandoned by its original owner. Through that went Chicaree at his leisure, and on, and upwards till twenty feet away he was at the far doorway, again in sight of the sky.

Chicaree rested a little, got his breath, then cautiously popped his head out of the back door. The dog at the front entrance was making terrifying sounds of heavy breathing, when not actually belching out his hate in loud explosive barks. It was so funny that Chicaree chuckled gleefully, to see that huge senseless brute digging away, digging himself in, playing Chicaree's own game really. For the squirrel watched cautiously and joyfully, as, little by little, the dog got deeper in. When at last nothing was to be seen but his coarse waving tail, the squirrel knew that *his* chance had come.

He slipped out quietly, in cover of the weeds, and sped away to the grove. From a high limb he saw the cur still digging and barking into the den, and he sent his own ringing defiance across the meadow. ' *Snick, Snick, Snick, Snicker, Chic-a-reeeeeeeeeeeeeeeeeeeeeeeeeeeeeeeeeeeeeeeeeeeeeeeeeeeeee.*'

The dog knew nothing of it, and continued his mad attack on the woodchuck citadel. But another squirrel made response ' *reeeeee* '; and bounding from limb to limb she came, his mate. They rubbed noses and twiddled their whiskers in affectionate greeting. Then as she did, her keen nostrils told her that he had found that alluring prize, the rare red russula; it was strong on his breath. It made her mouth water; she too loved the famous delicacy. Eagerly she looked about to see if he had brought her a share. But he was so intently watching the dog that he did not realize her tense interest in the smell of their rarest food. Her snuffing and searching did not seem to interest him. She felt neglected and peevish, that she was to be tantalized by the scent of the russula that he seemed to have enjoyed, while she had no part in the feast. She left him with petulant haste.

He followed, and tried to please her with caresses. She bounded away still faster ; and in response to every advance, showed yet more plainly that she resented his evident selfishness.

At last she reached the home den, an old flicker-hole high in an oak, and once inside—she did not slam the door, for there was no door—she turned and showed her teeth in menace ; which is plain squirrel talk for ' You keep away ; I don't want you in here '.

Poor Chicaree ! He had barely escaped with his life and now he was forced into an utterly unnecessary domestic brawl.

The injustice of it hung over him like a cloud. He went through the woods to the stream, got a good draught of water ; he looked about for food, found plenty of the ordinary kinds—nuts, seeds, fruit in abundance, for it was late summer. But the forage he most desired he found not. There seemed not another red russula on earth. He wandered off and climbed to a high look-out, whence he could see the battle-field. His enemy was there, but plainly tired of it, for he was not digging but sitting looking at the hole, evidently puzzling over it.

Chicaree could not resist it; he sent a long challenge across the meadow. The cur turned his eyes towards the woods, but did not leave the hole, in which he was sure he had a red squirrel cooped up.

Chicaree thought, no doubt, that by this time his wife's fit of temper might have passed. He climbed to the nest. She heard the scratching of his claws, and met him at the door with a savage snarl as before. So he leaped to a distant limb, travelled far away to a sunning-perch, and stretched himself out.

After a time, he picked a fine green hickory nut in the juicy pulp stage, and climbed the home tree. He put his head in the door, with the peace-offering. Her response was an angry snort that scared him nearly off the tree; and he hurried away.

He had nothing to do now, but watch the cur at the hole. The sun had swung quite low, and at last the dog went slowly back to the farmhouse.

Then Chicaree bethought him of a plan. Cautiously going to the edge of the woods, and then to the last tree, he peered across. He could see the farm dog now by the kitchen door; and after a final scrutiny, he rippled down the farther side of the trunk. Keeping cover as long as he could, he made for the place where he had lost that fateful titbit.

There it was, a little dried at the broken edges now, but he hastily crammed his mouth full. Then seizing the largest reddish piece of the broad rich cap, he bounded back to the woods; straight to the home tree and the home he went. He scratched noisily up the trunk; he wanted her to know he was coming. He poked his head into the hole with the prize in advance.

The angry little ' *chirr* ' inside was cut short. He tumbled in beside her; she seized the luscious peace-offering, and revelled in its aromatic joys. For a time there was no sound but the munching of their jaws, followed by a low soft *coo* as they snuggled up together and went to sleep.

156

XI

The Woman Bear

I LOVE that good old Indian way that speaks not of 'she wolf' or 'she bear', but of 'woman wolf' and 'woman bear'; surely the redman has a little closer got than we to the big rock-bottom thoughts of the live things' brotherness.

I wish I dared tell of the lover meeting of the Bears, the ponderous caressing, the unimagined amoration on the mountain-side, as I sense it in my memory's life again. The resonant grumbling, anger, menace, ecstasy—I know not what. I felt only intensity, emotion, hankering, animality, and the two huge bulks, dim lighted in the forest gloom; and the thuds—love-pats maybe, but pats that surely would have crushed a lesser brute to earth, and yet, left out, would hint indifference.

And when the moon dies out and comes again, we note, if we be of the woods, that the big Bear's track is all alone, and that the lesser mighty brute moves all alone on a lower level now.

157

See that huge imprinted naked foot; heels, toes, but seldom claws. How seldom claws—till we find the log ripped open, the tall tree raked.

See the ponderous track from anthill to lily-bed; pigpen to beehive; mouse's nest to grain field; sheepyard to apple tree; salmon run to huckle bush; trailing vine to crawling bug—quirked, swung, hidden, heedless, but ever purposeful. Food, food, the one big urge!

And growth with every moon.

Oblivious, content, uplifted, alone, blind, sordid, earthy. Alone, alone and glad to be alone she was; as Hagar went alone when her biggest happening was near.

Oh, sting divine; oh, holy torment; that by pain and wrench can raise and glorify!

Oh, blessed, long-forgotten ecstasy that incubates!

Oh, tiny pollen of the big event to be!

Oh, three times sacred litany unwrit!

I have heard her in the night, as she sniffed analysis of instance on the wind.

I have seen the winding zigzag of the rounded

toes when mapped she out the woods ; and I think I know the tree she marked, though I do not know why she marked it.

Oh, huge-haired Woman Bear ; who told you that the snow was near ? And then at hand the climax that shall change your lead to gold ?

The big uprooted pine, the caverned bank, the casual jetsam bush, the rime above the snow, the nimbus of unusualness, the exhalation frozen—all, all that whisper tales.

Oh, I have seen it, and a little learned to read it.

Older than writing ; older than speaking ; wordless whispers.

The Big Thing has come ; the wondrous happening, for which no cost was counted. The same as when our world broke from the sun.

Crystal white the chamber of the bliss elected, and all her lead is turned to gold. Irradiancy, if our eyes could see, would flame a halo round the upturned root. The wild things see and read ; the moose swings off ; the hunting wolf glides silent by with glowing eyes ; the twitterers hush and scare and shun.

Dark Age painters dared to paint it on canvas—that radiance.

But the huge root hides its tidings ; the rumour runners of the pine top are leash-held ; waiting.

Piling snow, piling snow ; frost and piling snow. Two trees may hide the forest, as one cloud may hide the day ; but still the day is there in all its corrosive effulgence. The day-folk know its nearness, its inevitable, endwhile overmastery.

The sharp snow stang no more on the winds ; the trees burst not at night with frost, the loud disintegrator.

The titmouse plumes his cap of jet and sings : ' Spring soon.'

The flattening snow is weeping out its short white life.

The all-mother, brown-complexioned, shows her face.

The fur bulk in the cave, long curled about a sacred something—a double something—heaves, rises responsive to the in-wind call, to the wood-world call of awakening ; turns ; looks. But tiny voices quell all other impulse, demand and

The Woman Bear

win absolute loving allegiance ; she obeys, yearning and hankering. She curls again above them to consecrate her everything to them ; loving the slavery ; yearning for larger sacrifice.

Many times the sun must rise, and the snow must go from the deepest hollows in the shade ere she will risk her darlings' feet.

Were ever things so gently precious, so fragile, as these two round and rolling forms ?

How she dreads to see their feet endangered on a cold or wet place !

How vigilant is she to place her body between them and all seeming danger !

How ready to screen from sun or wind or rain !

And when the way seems rough or hard, or the pace has tired their pudgy limbs, she is fain to lean against a tree and, woman-wise, make a lap of her huge knees, where they can scramble up and be warmed, both feet and body, as they feed.

And ever this loving holy animalism grows stronger and bigger as they grow, till they begin to find the world of other foods.

This maybe is climax that foretells the waning ; but even when they grow too big to hang on either arm or even for that yearning lap, she knows no better bliss, no other bliss than this : to loll back and swing her muzzle with a sort of hankering whine, with a look of yearning love as she holds them to her ; holds tight, on each side one ; clutches even to their hurting ; throwing back her head and pushing forward her breast for the joy of feeling their nudging noses, in her eagerness to be their need, to give, to send the best of all her being into them.

Animal ?
Brutal ?
Maybe so.
But this, I tell you, is the very same feeling, half selfish, half sacrificial, that our own women find in the hankering of motherhood ; the joy of possessing, touching, nursing, the little ones born of their bodies.

XII

The Lovers and the Shining One

A Rede by the Singing Woodsman

BLACK slats and masts of trees ; glinting water between at times ; slushing sounds at the far-away margin ; a soft sweet tinkle of the song sparrow in some blackness ; more slushing noises ; a little *chirr, chirr* ; whistling pinions overhead, gone unexplained—and there was slushing in the margin. Squattering of some duck-bird in the farther gloom, but louder slushing there was in the near margin, and a *chirring* of intercommunion ; moving water making zigzag glintings, and confluent blots of near black tree boles ; and a louder slushing close by in the margin.

Then silence, the night-walker senses intrusion.

Then dead silence.

A loud *sniff*.

Be wise, oh intruder ! Be inhumanly gentle, oh human watcher ! Give off no emanation of

fear, be calm. Give off no scent of effort, be stock-still. Give off no air-throb, even of hand-wave, nor head-turn; be as frozen.

The prowler may scent you. He will. He may size you up as a neutral, unless by emotion your irradiants are tinctured, and so are made hostile.

SPLASH, SPLASH ! ! ! how it strikes the tense nerve like a blow on a harp-string, like midnight crash of some book on piano keys, like a blow on the cords of one's hammock. A river-horse plunging you think, but no, it is only a muskrat, a muskrat, much less than a rabbit. What a big black sound it seems in the big wide night. Now there is a dullness prevailing.

Have you learned the first rule, the rede of the woodwise: When doubtful turn into a statue, be as frozen. There is safety in freezing. Have you seen the wise cottontail baffle most dangers ? Then have you seen that his game is this : *freeze, freeze*. Lay low when in doubt; keep silence in danger. This is the rede of the underbrush; this is the deft of the trailwise.

That ton of rock that avalanched into the pool was only a three-months-old muskrat, a muskrat as big as a kitten.

The Lovers and the Shining One

Wait, freeze, wait.

Whistling wings unexplainable passing, now dullness predominant ; but freeze.

The long snaky shades of the limb slats shake shorter. Still freeze. Feel you not the boring eyes, the sense measurement of another thought-centre. You are conscious strongly, and sensitive weakly. Yours is not the opalescent iris, therefore freeze, wait and freeze.

He has sized you up. They have sized you up. You are of an abominable kind, but maybe better than your kind, because you wait, freeze and wait.

What is that ?

No miracle. Such are of a bygone age—the blind and the mind-halt assure us. Oh, wonder of the welkin, what divineness is this ? How it saffronates the blessed firmament with mellowing effulgency. It upfloods, possessing, intensing. Oh, eye-soothing shimmer ! Oh, good irradiance ! Oh, harbinger foreglow of some strong one burning behind the hill ! How good it is to be alive with eyes to see it. There ! Ho, it comes ! They call it the Moon—that high glory, only the Moon ! It comes up. How glad I am for such a beautiful miracle. See how it eats holes in the eastern trees.

165

How it burns through them, abolishing the lesser limbs in its way.

Hush ! Can you not feel it ? Can you not sense that you are being sensed ? Very close now.

Cease your cheap mental jangling, quell those overhammered strings, conjure a mental hush ; you have forgotten.

That blessed bright one is up higher ; her twin sister in the water now, going down as she goes up.

Round the tree boles are sheets of broken glass, now they sparkle and crawl.

See where the long wires of the red willow are entangled, they make a foolish prison for the Shining One. She burns them, they are forgotten.

The lines that sparkle, crawl. When mud and crystal meet, they sparkle ; where stolidity meets limpidity, they crawl.

But wait, freeze, wait.

That squattering on the far bank ? No, that is nothing. That scratching on a trunk so placed to make ye moon-blind ? No, that is little Shaka Skandaway, the Flying Squirrel. When they kill him and put his skull in a museum, they call him *sciuropterus*, but here he is Shaka Skandaway.

Hush !

Chirr-chirr. They are talking.

Does your heart thump ? Surely. They are talking of you. They are deciding. *Chirr-chirr.* You are of no account they agree. You are negative, negligible.

Other noises. All remote. Other things living their lives. Only these close at hand are restrained.

Wait, freeze, wait.

Chirr-chirr-girrr.

Keep still, emanate friendliness.

The big golden arc-light swings higher.

Why does its golden light make all the world so blue ?

See that blue bank by the moving blue water !

See the glorious blue vigour of that skunk cabbage !

Hush ! What is that dusky bigness, that blots out the skunk cabbage ? How big ! How dusky ! It has little blueness. But see ! The dull bigness moves this way, and two red lamps are shining. It is like a motor-car coming. Yes, you had heard of it, but you did not know it was so. They were vain words to you.

Now you know : the lamps of the prowler. Now they are gone, now one appears, now two. They are gone.

But see, there are four. What ! They separate now. Two bulks of soft bigness.

They pause by the water. They break its blue greyness into glintings and fire. When they dabble, it sparkles out light, little lightnings, faint fireflies.

They come nearer.

Jammed against the tree-trunk, rugged and rough as a tree-trunk, are you, waiting, rigid, waiting.

How you long to sweep the mosquitoes from your face. They are not many but bloodathirst. You must not move. A hand-lift would mean hostility.

The big dusky prowlers turn the red lamps on you. They gaze. They turn aside and stand angling. What are they doing ? They give the signals. The black mask, the banded tail—their tribal flag, the badge of the Coon-raccoon folk.

They are signalling : Who are you ? friend or foe ?

Hush—wait. You have answered, you did not know it, but you emanated the answer ' Friend '. That is enough.

Wait. They lamp you, they break dull water into sparkles ; they slush along the shore, they melt softly. They leap on a frog ; they squelch him. (Wait—keep still—keep freezing.) The bigger one has him. The lesser complains. The bigger one drops the meat. The lesser one washes and eats it. The lesser one digs muttering, then grabs in the mud—a small eel, and chews it, washing off the muck, regales : the big one looking on. Then in the greenish-blue slime he swats a crawfish. The lesser one claims it. He yields uncomplaining. The lesser one *sniffs* apprehensively ; then he comes red-eyed toward you. He rumbles in his chest. Why ?

This is what he says : ' Do not at your peril molest *her*.'

Oh, you have guessed their secret. Is it not beautiful, brutish and beautiful ?

You wait, freeze, and wait.

The two big blots of movableness are gone, softly sunk in the interlacement. Very quiet.

Oh, be glad for the Moon. For a long time after, you will remember how brightly it shone to-night. And in the morning you will see tracks on the margin, not very big, but tracks of bare hands and feet, eight of them.

XIII

The Rat and the Rattlers
A Study of an Animal Personality

THE Rat—how we all hate him, insidious, pertinacious—two keen chisels cutting all night, saw, saw, saw; food, woodwork, framework, metal-work; polluting, destroying, boring even into lead pipes, diffusing plagues, stinks and terror.

How he scares the children and their mothers! How every zoo is teeming with his kind! How the elephants fear him, and how he gnaws their huge, helpless toes as they sleep, and nicks their morbid trunk tips! He has even crawled into the trunk, and driven some huge beast mad with pain and fright.

How verminated is his coat! How fierce his endless hunger! How shamelessly cannibal!

How we all hate him!

Has, then, the Rat no honoured gift for human veneration?

171

Yes, indeed. Above all others that we men adore is one : the superexcellence of courage ; and courage he has in greater measure than any beast that meets him.

This you may do, abhor the Invisible Walker in the Night, and loathe his way ; but bow in reverent adoration of his gift, the pluck that never yields, the heart that never quails, the small dark soul that fronts a million foes without dismay.

In our woodshed, as everywhere, were Rats. I was a boy with hunter-trapper cravings growing in my little brutish mind.

I bored a hole in a board and set it around with long sharp wires, then nailed it on a baited keg so the wires all pointed in. At the other end I made an iron grating open, but very strong, that would claim a captive's thought and save some feeble part of the trap from his attack.

Early in the morning, my father broke my rest by shouting : ' What is that creature you have caged in the barrel ? '

Shivering in my shirt, I ran, and shivered more with trapper zeal as I saw the fierce, insistent rasping of the wires with blunted bloody teeth.

172

The Rat and the Rattlers

How animal I became ! I wanted to crush the captive, to let him run, to catch again, to tear with my teeth, to fondle the fur, and tear again. I did not understand. I did not then, nor did I till long after, when I saw a mink that tore the quivering body of a hare, then stroked and tore and lusted again.

What now with my captive ? Mine, mine, mine !

Yes, I remembered now the Rattlesnake Pillman. I knew him well, a strange man. Pills and poison sold he, but dreamily, for his heart was in the desert always. He was rough and rugged. Back of his wretched house was a wretched back yard. I can smell its foulness now—boxes and garbage, heaps of nameless filth, semi-harmless papers, boots and oyster-shells, a great glorious rank stramonium plant, splendid in its stinking vigour, royal in its venomousness—Caesarian, sinister, blooming, resplendent ; and just beyond, a deep, square, board-lined pit where the Pillman kept his darlings—four great Rattlesnakes, visible expression of unwonted convolution or reverted loop-lines in his strange, ill-centred brain.

Oftentimes I went to the Pillman.

I told him once of a garter snake that swallowed a small frog that squeaked as it went down. He listened intensely, with glowing eyes—but did not speak.

I took him a dead baby Skunk. He cut out its musk-sac, and preserved it as a treasure—but said nothing.

I killed a phoebe-bird with a stone, and his eyes glared in anger—but he spoke not.

I told him of a meadow-lark that sprang in the air to fling his very soul on the driving wind for the very gladness of being alive. His face worked, his eyes rolled, and he gasped, 'My God!'

I think he was an eagle in some other life.

I had hung my young chin often on the rim of his snake pen; I had unhygienically sucked the board-edge many times as I lingered to watch them ooze around.

I knew he fed them living prey, so I trundled my keg and captive to his store.

He was pleased, for he gave a little sniff-laugh. He raised the end-board of the keg, and put in an old shoe. The Rat scrambled into it to hide.

174

teased it with a stick till it faced about, then
it squirmed, its tail came out the open toe.
ith tongs, he seized the tail and held the victim
th its shoe, downhung.

Fierce those rasping teeth, undaunted that small
hting heart, and the Pillman said : ' He might
l one of my darlings before they can kill him.'

from his shop he took a dentist's forceps.
kept the shoe tight pinched, so the Rat was
d and helpless. The Pillman could not draw
ose teeth, but he broke them off and filed the
inters smooth.

Then to the Rattlers' pen we went. The day
s burning hot. The Rattlers buzzed, and
wled, and danced their tongues. Very hungry,
this was their time ; and the four long, slid-
, mottled bands with faded, blemished rainbows
ot a-moving, casting unfavourable eyes on each
ier, and moving, seeking.

They knew his step. Each flat, vile head was
ed—the split tongues dancing, the eyes with
l-bale glinting.

Thud, and the toothless Rat was in among them,
e the lead-armed gladiator sent to fight Com-
odus.

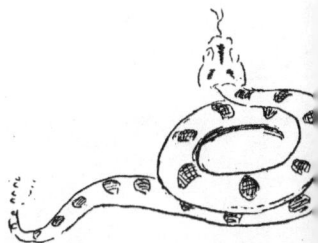

175

With the quick instinct of a fighter, he sprang to the semi-shelter of the angle-boards, and faced his foes.

Four great Rattlesnakes, active with the summer sun that sent their slug blood rushing.

Food, food, and heads up high they closed in oozily—feeling, reaching, recoiling at some slight alarm ; and the Rat faced this and that way, blinked at the bright sun, held back ; then when a Snake drew near, he sprang toward it, showing his toothless gums, and screamed defiance.

The Snake jerked back.

The others then flowed nearer, shunning just a little each his neighbour, like thugs distrusting each the other. They converged from every side. Poison was written in their every face, charged full their double fang-squirts were with loathsome spume that turns the red blood quick to vile and green putrescence in the veins.

Around they closed ; their glide and glint and eye unchanging spelt destruction—cold, sure and pitiless.

The Rat stood still.

They pushed their fore-ends forward, then, halting like inch-worms for the rear to overtake, they

raised their heads in conning towers of themselves ;
they glode, and ever the dancing tongues seem
tasting all the ambient air.

So they closed in crescentric.

This way and that way glanced the toothless
dauntless Rat.

The four long necks towered near, the fourfold
death impending. Now almost in the range they
were. The Rat made a plunge, and sounded his
war-cry. One Snake flung back, and through the
gap the Rat went flying. The next Snake struck,
and missed, for he was not coiled.

Then, in the next square corner, the Rat faced
as before. Again the shrinking, bold and shrinking, crescent of his foes. Again the charge, again
the Rat escaped, and ever round the four-square
pen.

But it must end ; there was no final safety for
the fangless one. His strength was spending fast
with all this lengthened hunt ; and as he leaped
with lessened speed, a Rattler struck. The fangs
bit home, the spawn of speedy pestilence was
spewed into the wound. Death's strangle-hold
was on the Rat.

His last hope gone—did he lose heart ? Not

for the faintest fraction of a pulse-beat. Now was he doomed ; but rose in him the spirit of his race. Doomed, yes—but never downed. Since all that he could do was die, he'd die as glorious as he might.

Shunned he no more those scaly split-faced flat-heads ; straight at his foremost foe he sprang. Just where the head and thinning neck are joined, he gripped with all his force. He ground that hateful, scaly rope with all the power of toothless aching jaws ; and crushed so the gaping, frothing head fell limp, and the tail buzzed out its death-cry.

Then at the next, the Rat. Receiving but heeding not a second deadly shot, he chewed with all the death-power of his hinder teeth across the Rattler's back. The reptile squirmed and struck, but writhed in agony with a broken back ; and the Rat rushed at the next. But the pestilence in his veins was spreading, blighting, corroding ; his blood was changing into thick green soup. His hind legs faltered now, yet gnashed he still his splintered bleeding gums. Helped by his dying paws, he tore the vent-hole open of the next, broke off the fiendish taunting rattle, and feebly lurched again, with glazing eye, with dragging paralysed hind limbs.   And in this last and desperate stound, he clamped his bleeding gums on his last foeman's throat, and squealed his final squeal of war ; and dying, clenched and broke the long thin neck, and limpened as he hung. Dead, dead on a field of dead ; not one was left.

The Pillman snorted like a horse when ye throw a bearskin on his back ; like a razorback at bay was he. His eye was blazing, his bony hands were griping :
' He has robbed me of my Rattlers !
' Gosh, how I hate him !
' Gosh, how I love him !
' Gosh, how I hate him !
' He has robbed me of my Rattlers ! '

XIV

Dipo : Sprite of the Desert

WHY do they call it desert ? A desert is commonly understood to mean a barren, burning land of hot winds and stifling sand-storms, deserted by all living things, even plants ; cheerless, dreary, appalling, and death-dealing.

It would be hard to get further from the truth than this if the Mohave is a true desert. Imagine a broad and somewhat level sandy plain dotted over thickly with low shrubs, chiefly sage and greasewood, with occasional cactus, and here and there scattering groves of palm-like yuccas, casual patches of greening herbs just thick enough to tinge the middle distance with their green or grape-like bloom, but melting into the golden haze that masks the upland where it, far off, butts starkly into towering, naked granite peaks of purple, shot with golden lights. Peaks that rise up, up, abruptly up, to bear, each high above his noble shoulders in the gentle blue, a crown of white—the crown without which

no mountain ever can be in the noblest rank, a cap of shining snow, a blazoned promise to mankind that this year the blessedness of water will not fail.

Yes, this is the desert at a hasty glance, the desert in its poorest time—the time of bleak and dusty winter winds. But spring comes here as well as anywhere ; and when the parsimonious rain has laid the dust, when the greasewood has begotten for itself a deeper green, when the corpse-like sage looks quick again, and the cactus, the reptile among plants, puts on a semblance of aliveness spelled in orchid terms, the deadly sand responds with a plain-wide sheen of flowers that beggars language to describe, blooms that numb the brain's perception with their exquisite multiplicity, their wondrous un-expectedness, their boundless gladness in the spring that they so delicately express ; not lush, not rank, not crowded, but everywhere in beds, groups, and little brotherhoods, that nothing in the world but perhaps the mountain meadows in July can equal for joyous profusion ; and nothing anywhere, not even the wide, unbroken fields of the deserted arctic summer plains, can faintly approach in the tender delicacy of each exquisite and low-hung bloom.

Nevertheless, this is only the frame of the picture, the setting of the jewel that really claims one's thought. For the desert is the home of higher things than flowers ; and every sandy place between the scattering blue-eyes or the low, flat loco-weed is pattered over with an endless, ever-changing maze of four-footed tracks and trails of living creatures.

There is no wild stretch of our land that for super-abundance of harmless, beautiful wild life can rank with desert zone. Africa may have a larger animal population on some parts of its tropic breadth, but that is a far-off country. In America, from Arctic to tropic, and from Atlantic to the sun-down sea, there is no place that can compare with the great Mohave Desert for the abundance and variety of its bright-eyed, fur-clad creatures. Every one of the millions of low bushes has a home in its roots, large or small, according to its owner's fashion, and marked with the owner's name and ways in characters that the desert hunter knows.

The hard or leafy forest floor of other lands betrays no sign of the mouse or fox that passed an hour ago, but the finely sifted desert sand tells all. Here on every side we see them, the chains of tracks, the hunter signs, the confluent trails that mark these little people's streets, and point out the well-worn thresholds of their open doors. Big and little, small and very small, they wind about, lead to the holes and feeding-grounds, or tell some story of their lives, their loves, their tragic ends.

Here in record of the foot-writing are cottontails, jack-rabbits, ground-squirrels, chipmunks, pack-rats, gophers, kangaroo-rats, calling-mice, deer-mice, lizards—harmless children of the sun, with their overlords, the coyote, the badger, the desert fox, the hawk, the raven, and the owl, and their Bolsheviki, the scorpion, the chuckawalla, and the deadly rattlesnake.

But with them, and rarer, better than them all, was a winding twin-foot, interlinking, wide-spread trail—the trail of a two-foot, and also a creature with a long important tail, the track of the kangaroo-rat, the big kangaroo of the desert.

What the brook-trout is to the mountain stream or the chamois to the Alps, what its bloom is to the rugged cactus or the petrel to the wide, salt sea, is the kangaroo-rat to the arid, shimmering, elusive deserts of the far South-west. She is as swift as drifting sand, painted with silver and gold like shining dust, filled with the joy of the great open spaces, happy in its foods, and contented in its drought. No need has she of water or of anything but burning sand. Its hard, dry plants are her food, its open levels her playground and her world. Her home, her sleeping-chamber, and her citadel is a burrow in the earth deep down in the bosom of the desert.

A million square miles of the hot, dry West is the range of her kindred ; but the hottest, dryest of it all, the great Mohave Desert and similar reaches, is the proper mould in which was cast this creature of the burning dust.

See that long, low mound, a score of paces around, with a mesquite thorn and a dozen grease-wood bushes scattered on its rounded top. This is the roof-tree of Dipo's home. The winding trails of twin-foot tracks are all about it, and lead in pathway multiplicity to an entering hole. There may be a dozen entrances, some of them open, some of them closed with fresh-heaped sand ; but all lead to the same labyrinthine burrow, which, in a sample taken for exact survey, was the work of years and of generations of the Dipos. Seventy-five feet long all told, its complex galleries began

185

at the ten entrances and twisted hither and yon, till a final low level of three and a half feet down was reached. There were seven various halls or chambers, twelve store-rooms, and three little toilets, serving the necessary rules of health and cleansing.

Only one nesting-den was there in all this, deep down at the lowest level of this under-world abode, the most protected by the mothering sand, and remotest from the heat and cold, the shock of heavy feet, or dangerous approach. It was a rounded chamber, a hand-span wide and high, lined with a great hollow globe of soft-chewed fibres of the plants about, and inner lined with curving feathers —turkey, guinea-fowl, and chicken—from the ranch-house in the distance, with bright-red feathers of the crimson linnet as a contribution from the wild things. From this three corridors furnished escape in case of actual invasion, but many other safeguards were there : blind alleys, trap-turns, false approaches, and stop-gaps of movable sand. Last of all, there was off this nest a little toilet for the family, that the exquisite home be not defiled.

Twelve small storehouses for food were made and partly filled in order that stormy weather or fierce frost—yes, frost, for it comes with winter on this

igh-up plain—may find the Dipo and her family
vell supplied indoors. For places of amusement
nd exercise were two big rooms, a winter hall, and
nder the strong, protecting roots of the mesquite
spacious room where a dozen of the kangaroos
light have met, and half a dozen played some
ame. An upright plunge-hole or ventilating-
aft near by, a store of food on one side, a toilet-
oom on the other, and six fire-escapes completed the
lan and equipment of this carrousel of the little folk
f the sand. Of the ten doorways, seven were open,
nd only three plugged with newly placed sand.

This is Dipo's home, refined, intricate, and, like
ll homes, a reflex of the owner. Her food is every
esert plant of the hundreds that grow within her
ange of a quarter-mile around her mound, save one
-the bright-green, stinking creosote. No desert
reature will touch it.

Her drink ? She has none, not as we understand
. Yet the morning sand in level places shows
hundred little pockets dug by the paws of this
xquisite night-prowler. They are not accidents,
r they are many and regular. The diggers
ere not seeking for seeds, for seeds are best
und on the surface ; nor for roots, because the

187

signs are in open places far from plants with roots. There can be no doubt that these little prospect-holes are made in a search for insects of which there are many kinds buried down an inch or two ; and these big, fat, hard-shelled, juice-filled creatures are to the desert kangaroo what the can of tomatoes is to the throat-parched cowboy—meat and refreshing drink, but especially drink. Therefore the Dipo digs in the sand not for food, but for drink, her only drink. Dry, bone-dry, though her country is, her loved and only beverage is *bug-juice*, rich and strong.

The desert child has two strange equipments for her special life. On her back, between the shoulder-blades, she bears the battery of a wireless telegraph, combined with a rubber-stamp and ink-pad with which she stamps her name, when record of the same may help her friends. It is merely a big, round gland that yields to the air a faint musky smell that, on the night air, far away, lets any kinsman know that such a one is passing, and is near or far up-wind. Or, when she gently presses this shoulder-pad on a low-hung root or overhanging rock, it is to all her exquisite, discriminating kind a simple notice easily read that such and such a one was here.

Dipo : *Sprite of the Desert*

Very wide are these open spaces of the dry upland.
or miles and miles there is no landmark. Only
e unvaried sage and the scattering mesquite, each
ke the last ; and if a towering yucca shows its head
ar, it is only one of a thousand similar towering
eads. So Dipo, travelling in the starry night,
andering in pursuit of alluring new foods or play-
g· hop-scotch with her merry clan, or, last and
orst, flying homeward in desperate haste from
ndit coyotes or hush-winged owls, might easily
iss her unmarked way. But for this she has a
onderful special gift, a compass that, it seems,
s never failed her. Very broad at the ears is her
wn-brown head, and that great added bulk comes
ot from ear-bones bigger than is common, but
om a pair of road-guides, bony mechanisms, filled
ith strange fluids, floating needles, and delicate
rves, a new machine, a road-recorder, a gyro-
ope in short, bestowed in order that this night
anderer on the unmarked plains may never miss
r way.

Thus we have learned of the place and home of
is exquisite prowler in the dark, this living jewel-
wer of the rugged desert plain, of her house and
r foods, of her new strange weapons for the life

KANGAROO RAT

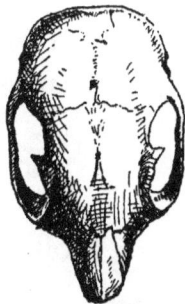

RED SQUIRREL

battle that she daily fights. But who can adequately show the dainty little soul within, the wild and gentle spirit that peeps from those big soft eyes? Without teeth or claws or ferocity to fight, her only safety from a multitude of foes is her great speed— her speed and her kindly mother, the desert, ever ready to receive and hide her in her bosom. These are all, and this the proof that they are enough : for her race still lives and prospers, as it always did. Not even man, disturbing, interfering, upsetting, has turned the balance so it does her harm.

Seeking the peace of the desert—for in the desert is peace—he came, the wanderer from the East, and found and loved it. Its friendly spirit entered in, possessed him ; therefore he loved the desert things. Then he came to the mound with its complex tale of life. The noon wind had levelled off the sand. The nightly spread of myraid trails was wiped out, but the little doorways were there, with the dim upleading pathways. And he gazed as one who for the first time sees a precious scroll or thing of beauty that he has read of and dreamed of for years.

Yes, such a little thing can deeply move, if the soul is sensitive and long preparing.

He kneeled and gazed. This way and that he sought, and learned but little more than this—that here was verily the place, here was the home of the desert's fairest living thing. But nothing more he saw, for the sprite is absolutely vowed to a life of starlight only.

There was one way open for more knowledge, and with a sense of almost wickedness he took it. By that sand-closed door he set a big spring cage trap, baited with oatmeal, raisins, and cheese, for he knew not which might be to the night one's taste.

And coming in the morning, the wanderer had a thrill, yes, three thrills, almost shocks; and he knew not which was strongest, the treasure-trove feeling, the joy of hunter's success, or the shame of sacrilege. For here in one corner of the cage was the most exquisitely beautiful thing he had ever seen in fur. Bright-yellow plush was its mantle, with white satin gloves, slippers, and vest. It had great liquid eyes, like those of a gazelle, and a long striped tail that ended in a banneret of white.

The wanderer had some book-won knowledge of the wild one's looks, and yet he felt a sense of intense surprise. Why do the books give a map of the body and no hint of its beauty ? Why do they offer measurements of the limbs, and close the eye to their grace and strength ?

Home to the ranch-house they went, wanderer, trap, and sprite. In the farthest corner of the trap she crouched ; and her big innocent eyes took in the wanderer's every move, with fear, wonder, gentleness, and a childishness that was touching. The wanderer reached in a slow, firm hand and seized the fawn-eyed sprite. She struggled a little, but made no attempt to bite, and uttered no sound. He transferred her to a cage almost big enough for a man, and here the wild one had the freedom of a prisoner who leaves his cell to walk in the prison-yard.

She sailed across and around, high on two hind legs, with her white hands pressed on her white bosom and her tail curved up behind her. Round once or twice she went, sketching on the sanded floor the familiar, linking twin-foot trail of the nightly desert. Then seeing no way out, she leaped straight up, not once, but half a dozen times at half a dozen places ; but only bumped her head. Escape was impossible. Then she settled down in one corner to watch the fearsome monster who held her in his power. How she hated him, how she feared him ! How could she know that he loved her ?

Wise monster, wise wanderer, he was ; for, bent on taming her, he began, as the Indian says, ' making medicine with his mouth '. He talked softly, cooingly to the captive, and very slowly and softly reached forward his hand. At the slightest sign of fear or move to escape, he stopped still, but kept on gently telling the wild one that he was her friend.

Each knew nothing of the other's speech ; but back of speech is always the spirit, the soul sense, that lives in the language, and is the same in all, however different their sounds may be.

The animal mind had long been the wanderer's study, and he knew that the desert sprite was getting his soul sense through the words which in them-selves meant nothing to her. She was sensing his utter friendliness. When that should overcome and cast out fear, she would receive him as a friend. And this came far more quickly than with any other wild thing he had met. The liquid eyes lost their hint of wild terror, the vibrant whiskers ceased to tremble at last, as the wanderer gently stroked the prisoner's head and called her ' Coooee ', ' Coooee ',

13   193

which was meaningless, only it was the right kind of sound to act as carrier of the gentleness he felt toward her. And then she surrendered very slowly, but completely. She no longer shrank away. Her head bowed a little forward, so he could the more easily stroke her gold-brown hair. The big eyes, which had bugged with fear, now softened, and the eye-lids, sleepy, drooped.

By these signs he knew that they had reached a friendly understanding. But there was one more proof that was needed : would she accept his gifts ? Would she eat from his hand ?

No food was near. He dared not call to his friends to bring this or that, for the rude and clanging change of voice vibration and sense undertone would have undone all his gains. There was nothing for it but a slow, gentle retreat. She started as his hand left her head. Her whiskers vibrated like wireless tentacles taking in some jarring overcharge. He stopped still, and spun a little magic thread with whispered ' cooing ', and slowly withdrew his hand from the cage. Everything he did was slow. Chesterfield has told us, ' You cannot be polite in a hurry.' Politeness is kin to gentleness, and this exquisite creature of the under-world must find in her captor nothing but the most refined politeness, or their friendly acquaintance would end at once.

He was careful not to jar the cage or the chair or the door as he went out. He hated his shoes for their discordant squeaking as he came back with samples of all the eatables he could find, and like an assorted meal he slowly pushed them in, not on a saucer, but in the hollow of his hand ; for, as he thought, she must remember his hand as a giver of good things.

Much of the taming was undone by his going away and by the jarring of the cage as the door was opened ; but the magic of the kind intention, entwined with the gentle voice, won another little victory over her fears. Soon again he was stroking that velvety back, and in a few minutes she was eating the peace-offering he held out in his other hand.

This was going far ; yet there was one more step, a better proof. Would she come at call ? Was the sound of his voice not a scare, but a lure ?

This he never was to teach her, for all that night he heard her pattering up and down the cage or leaping high in a fruitless, endless trying to get out.

The soothing little magic he could make with soft talking was gone as soon as he went ; therefore when next the sunset came, he gently took the captive to a far-off spot in the sage and cactus and set her down. She gazed blankly at the new freedom. He touched her. She sat still as a bump of golden sand, not believing. He clapped his hands as a magician does to end a trance or break a spell. She sprang to her height, then sailed away over sage and sand-heap, to be lost to view in her own dear native realm, to be folded again in her mother's arms and bosom, to meet her mate and friends, again to live her desert life.

The fire-ball sun has set behind the Bernardino peaks. The purple of the eastern sky flows down like a flood of wine, and fills the wide basin of the desert, first in the hollows, then over the flats, and later one by one the higher spots, till all are overwhelmed.

The singing coyote and the dancing owl are out already, though they reckon themselves of the night-folk, and the afterglow is still strong behind the peaks. But the purple overcomes the gold, the stars are lit, the big bright kind that are not seen in other lands. It is night.

196

Of all the creatures of the desert night, the Dipo seems most insistent on its very gloom. Not a vestige of even twilight will she willingly accept. Of all the thousands whose tracks are daily found, not one in fifty is seen in hours of light. Those that are met on the prairie are seen after nightfall by the sudden light of a motor-car. Not a few are killed at such times, for the blazing light dazzles and confuses them beyond the power of quick escape. More than one observer has noted that a light attracts them, and they may be captured by a combination of jack-light and net. This is indeed a failing of all true night-folk.

In some wise way the peoples of the under-world seem to know when the gloom they love is on the upper life; and forth from her deep-down nest at the right time comes the desert-rat, followed, jostled, or led by her mate. She digs and pushes her way through the sand-pile barricade.

For a moment they peek from the hole. They venture out with a timid hop. They sense the breeze, they listen, they smell, they peer. A wild cat or a coyote may be just behind the bush that is their roof-tree. That crooked root may be a rattlesnake. But the coast is clear. They dig the door-

197

way free of sand-bars, and each in a different direction sets out to forage.

When a small boy raids an orchard he begins
eating a selected apple, but quickly stuffs as many
as possible into his pockets, and makes ready to dash
for safety the moment there is any alarm. This is
the jumper's method when she goes forth to seek
her meat. Hopping high, like a kangaroo, on two
legs, balanced by her tail, taking an extra high hop
at times to look around—' Stop, Look, and Listen '
is her watchword—she arrives at the feeding-
ground, ever farther from her home as the near
supply is used up. Desert shrimps, which are grass-
hoppers on the half-shell, serve for fish ; with flat
anisocoma, evening primrose, and little borage for
greens, and mashed caterpillars as meat course.
Leaves of wild mustard and water-leaf furnish
delectable salad, berries and beans of many kinds
are unexcelled for dessert.

She has sampled both flesh and fruit courses, when
a suspicious odour on the open sand causes her to
halt. Her tiny paws set the sand flying in little
jets between her spread hind legs as she digs with
gleeful certainty to another fat grasshopper, and
gobbles it with champing jaws that set her juices

running. Quite out of order, for this is shell-fish, and she has begun the dessert. But the bill of fare is not printed. At one or more places she thought she smelled other buried treasure, and sank little prospect-holes without success. But she passed on lightly, sensed the trunk of a tall creosote, rubbed her back ink-pad on it to let her mate know she had been there, leaped high in the air to take a look around, and had the ill luck to catch the eye of a foraging screech owl. In a moment the big, silent air-marauder had swooped her way. But the jumper is alert. In two leaps she is under a shelter-ing cactus, where she is safe ; and at once she drums with her hind feet on the sand, a danger-signal for her mate and kinsfolk—a signal whose timely warn-ing makes them perfectly safe. And the baffled owl goes careering afar, to try some more promising field.

Dipo is no more upset by the incident than is the visitor at a zoo when the caged leopard makes a futile slap at him through the distant bars. Hoppity-hop she goes on her two long legs, with her tail as curved balance. She keeps her dainty, white-gloved hands tight against her chest as she bounds, for they serve as hands and as diggers, but

never as feet, except on rare occasions, when, boy
like, she goes on all fours. The seeded spearhea
of a grass attracts her eye. It smells tempting
Good luck ! The seeds are still in it. With vibran
nose and lips, team-working to her teeth and daint
paws, she threshes the little harvest then and there
and the seeds, except for the samples used as test:
are stored in her ample cheek-pouches. Alread
these contain other seeds and a number of deliciou
leaves, but never so far as known are they used t
carry insects, berries, or any squashy food. Wha
would the furry lining be like if such untidines
were indulged in ?

Making a long cast to seek new forage, and a hig
hop for observation, she sees a strange-lookin
object, like the moon on the ground, a mass c
brightness, with wavy things, like red grass, risin
from it, and huge living creatures moving or lyin
about it.

She is drawn closer to it, fascinated by the strang
glare of the camp-fire. She draws nearer, and :
more fascinated. She gazes and comes closer, for
getting all sense of danger, when her eye catche
sight of a huge creature like an overgrown coyote
It is gazing at the bright wonder of the fire. The

by chance the coyote creature rises and rambles toward her. A sense of danger breaks the spell of the blazing wonder. Dipo turns, and lightly hops away, till all sign of the camp-fire is lost.

Now a distant rumble, a drumming made by some kinsman's foot, warns her to look out. On the ground under a prickly thorn she sinks down, a mere sand bump on the sand. There was a slight swish; and the form of a desert fox, immense in the dim sage, glides through the opening and goes on.

With easy hops of half a yard the jumper heads up-wind for a while, to get off the fox's beat. And then across an open space she catches a flash of white. Friend or foe? In the desert it is mostly foe. Again the flash, a white lantern swung like a yard-man's bull's-eye in a great half-circle, the national sign of her own people—the white tail tip swung to let the other know. She swings her own tail, then stamps. The answer comes—the same. She rubs her back pad on a low limb, then goes, rabbit-like, around; the other does the same. Thus they exchange places without coming near each other. Each smells the new rubbing-place. Then they must have laughed, for they are mates. Dipo hops up to her mate ; they twiddle whiskers, lick lips, and rub cheeks in friendly salutation.

But even as the pair caress and frolic on the sand they hear the grind of heavy feet, a sniff; and from the near sage springs a coyote big enough to block the sky, and swifter than an owl.

Her mate bounds backward, darting under the monstrous enemy. She leaps under a friendly bush. Alas ! it is only a grass tussock. The coyote knows it, and lands on top ; but Dipo jumps, eludes him, and springs away. Now it is a race on the open plain, and now is seen how the jumper can bound. Three feet in the air, five feet at a bound, five bounds to the second, she goes. The coyote is close behind at first, but the big brute must go nearly straight, while Dipo strikes a new sharp angle at nearly every jump, here, there, back, and forth, but making ever for home. In all the darkness of the night and the sameness of the sage, she never misses her way. The coyote races and follows for a hundred yards, then loses sight of the jumper. And she, wisely refraining from any high hop now, goes skipping like a cottontail under the bushes and cactus, till the foe is left far behind. Then speeding up her foraging-hops without spy-hop or observation or landmark, thanks to the twin gyroscope that her mother had given her, unerringly she reaches home.

On the edge of the tall timber greasewood, ten hops from the den, she halts, and thumps with her hind feet. On a low limb, which is their visitors' book, she writes her name with the pad on her back, looks well around, then swiftly moves homeward. No, her mate is not there. She closes the door by scratching back the sand, then empties her cheek-pouches in a store-room, and has a quiet bite before retiring.

Every night of their lives they have some such adventures as these. He is late, but she is not worried ; he can take care of himself.

She curls up to sleep. Presently she is awakened by a scratching sound outdoors. She runs to the hallway, thumps three times with her hind feet. The signal is answered. She digs on the inside, and he on the out. Her mate comes in. They twiddle whiskers and lick lips ; they close up the door with sand. After that, curled up together, they sleep in peace and perfect safety far underground in their cosy bed of chewed yucca fibre.

XV

Hank and Jeff

A group of hunters about the camp-fire they were —and one spoke about swapping dogs, much as he would horses or cows. Then a silent man growled out : ' No man ever gave up his dog—if it was really truly his dog.'

This struck a chord of memory in my heart, and I told this tale as it came to me long years before.

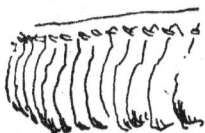

IT was in the wild romantic days of eighty years ago, when the Ohio River flowed through unbroken, glorious woods, when Kentucky was one great game-field. Here, on the lower Kentucky River, in his lonely cabin, lived Jeff Garvin, a grizzled old hunter, with no company but a big brindled bearhound whose name was Hank.

Very close were Jeff and Hank. Night and day their lives were the same. They shared the same food and the same perils. More than once when the hunter's arm had failed, it was staunch old Hank

that bore the brunt and saved him. Never once had they been apart from the day when first as a lubberly pup, Garvin carried him from the mother's kennel.

Their living came from the woods and streams ; deer, bear, and wild turkeys abounded. When they wanted meat, all Garvin needed to do was take down the trusty rifle, call Hank, and within a mile or two their wants were amply supplied.

In the winter, he trapped a few furs. These, with bear and buckskins, were swapped at the trading-store, twenty miles down the River, for powder, tobacco, tea, and such few things as the forest did not furnish for their needs.

In autumn, when the woods abounded in food, and the bears were fat, it was Garvin's custom to kill about twenty fine, black fellows, and smoke their hams for a food supply to carry him over next winter, spring and summer.

He was very expert at smoking hams. Garvin-cured hams were readily accepted by the trader on account. But a bear's ham is heavy, and four times heavy, when you must be your own pack-horse over twenty miles of rugged trail through heavy woods. The hams, therefore, were used at home, 'a specialty of the house', when rare strangers called, or a satisfying staple for himself and his dog.

It was in the fall of 1848. Garvin had stocked his smoke-house with twenty hams, mostly small, for these are best. The smoking had taken a month or more ; but now that the nights were cool, the meat was safe. Garvin let the fire go out, and enjoyed the vista of smoky hams that greeted the eye as he opened the heavy door. Very heavy was that door of hickory splits, and strong as the walls that made the smoke-house, for there were thieves to be reckoned with—not two-legged—in those days, man was the scarcest animal in the country, except woman—but four-footed robbers—nothing less than the bears themselves.

There was no reason to fear them when Hank and Jeff were in the neighbourhood, but the hunter and his dog were often away for a week at a time. Therefore, the smoke-house was built like a pier-dock, with heavy close logs over, under and around. On the roof was a smoke-hole with a hatch that was hung nearly balanced with a pulley rope. It stayed where placed for a while, but slowly settled down unless propped. It was closed at other times to

keep out small marauders ; the walls and overhang kept bears away.

It was early in November when Garvin went in to pick a ham for use. He was surprised to see that one of the pegs was empty. He counted the hams—there were but nineteen. He looked about carefully. There were no signs of burglary ; doors, walls and roof were all in perfect order. He searched about for tracks, but found none.

He called Hank. The dog was busy chewing an old bear skull, and came slowly.

'Here, Hank, smell him out Sic 'em. Where is he ?'

The dog obeyed, sniffed all about the cabin, and circled farther off ; then without apparent interest went back to the bear skull. Garvin was puzzled, and asked himself whether there were really twenty hams ; maybe he had miscounted. But no—all honest normal bears wear their hams in pairs, and here was an odd ham.

Their cabin door was only loosely closed at night. Hank slept on a bear-skin by his master's couch. At the slightest noise, he would get up, scratch the door open, and challenge or assail any creature, man or beast, that might on rare occasions come near.

seemed impossible for a burglar to enter the
ɪoke-house, which was close by. The mystery
as unexplained.

Three days later, Garvin entered the place and
und another ham gone. Again he sought for clues,
ʒain he and the dog searched all about for tracks.
ɪey found none, and soon Hank returned to an
d bear-hide that he had been chewing behind the
bin.

A few days afterwards, Garvin and Hank set out
wards the mountains on a preliminary trapping-
und, making a few deadfalls ready, so they would
: purged of the man-taint by rain, and weathered
fore the cold winter should come and make
ɪpping profitable.

That night, as they were about to turn in by the
mp-fire, they were aroused by the scream of a
nther not far away. They were familiar with
ɛse unearthly yells and quite unafraid. But there
ɪs a strange new note in this ; at times it was like
ɛ agonizing scream of a mad woman.

Hank rushed off, baying loud defiance to the
ɑllenge. And soon the sound of the baying
ʻund and the screaming panther died away.

Hank was gone so long that Garvin fell asleep.

14   209

In the morning, the dog was back, apparently un-harmed, but seeming dull and listless. Jeff offered him some venison, part of his own meal, but the dog seemed not hungry. He barely mouthed the juicy steak.

There was something disquieting about the whole affair. Garvin could not help remembering that an Indian devil was said to haunt these hills; and some of those yells were unlike any panther call he had ever heard.

Instead of going farther into the hills, he turned homeward, and by afternoon was back at his cabin. A general inspection showed another ham gone. Garvin was furious now. He scouted about for tracks, without success. He and Hank quartered the ground near and far, but they found nothing unusual. The smoke-house door was untouched, the house intact, and yet another ham was gone. There were no bear tracks or man tracks near, and Hank was much more interested in mauling that old bear skull with gritting teeth and rolling eyes than in searching for an impossible track.

That night, Garvin was deeply depressed. He cleaned his rifle, and smoked long and idly. He had heard often of spooks and warlocks in the

Hank and Jeff

Kentucky Mountains not so far away. He had heard of Indian Devils, Catamounts and Medicine Bears. And all of these weird creatures for once seemed almost real in the light of recent doings. For they seemed the only explanation of the continual losses and that uncanny voice.

Hank, too, seemed deeply moved by something of the sort. He curled his brawny brown form on the bear-skin as usual, and slept. But his sleep was broken with short whines and twitchings of his legs. Once or twice, he yelped as though in pain. So Garvin muttered at last : ' I wonder if that cussed panther hurt him, or maybe he's got spiked.'

He examined the dog's body and limbs, but found no injury. Hank responded to this care by licking his master's hand ; then curled up again for slumber.

But his sleep was broken and fitful as before. Garvin himself was wakeful. He sat up in his bunk, and something like superstitious fear possessed him as he watched the indomitable old bearhound tremble and whine in his sleep.

As Garvin stared uneasily, a thought came to him. ' That old Indian Medicine Man at Scioto put me up to a dodge that will tell what a dog is dreaming —a way to make you have the same dream.'

He reached for his big red bandanna hanging on a pair of deer horns, he softly spread it out on the head of the sleeping hound, left it for five or ten minutes ; then, lying flat on his back, he spread the bandanna on his own face.

He fell asleep and dreamed that he was a dog, that indeed he was Hank, the companion of the bear hunter. He dreamed that he rose from his bearskin in the night, went softly to his master's bunk, poked his moist snout in the face of the sleeping man, listened for a time, then softly went to the cabin door. Deftly opening it, he made for the smoke-house.

Six feet away was a tall pine-stump. He leaped on this, then with a mighty spring landed on the roof of the smoker. Near the top was the hung hatch. He thrust his nose under the edge and raised it ; then reached his long powerful neck and plucked the nearest ham from its peg, drew it through the smoke-hole, then down and away.

The hatch closed of its own weight. He carried the plunder off to a cedar swamp some forty rods away, and there feasted to repletion on the meat he loved the most. He could not eat it all ; and what was left, he buried in the black muck, digging a

hole with his paws but rooting the earth back with his nose till the meat was covered.

Garvin slept late. When he awoke, the dog was still on the rug. The door was a little open, which might mean that the dog had been out chasing some prowling beast. For, though Hank could open the door, he never was known to shut it. And often-times, the door was left open all night, so that proved nothing.

His dream was strong upon him as Garvin went out. He opened the smoke-house to find *another ham gone.* His lips were tight, his jaw set, as he glanced toward the cabin, to note that Hank was again mauling the old bear skull as though that were to blame. Garvin went on alone to the cedar swamp. He saw Hank watching, even while pretending to maul the skull.

Every stump and tree was familiar through his dream, and he went direct to the cedar bush. There were signs of recent disturbance. He dug fiercely with his fingers. Soon he unearthed a bone —then another—bear bones—ham bones—then— part of the last ham !

He stood up straight. He gasped, ' My God.' He glanced furiously toward the cabin, and gave a familiar whistle. But no Hank came joyously bounding. He strode quickly back, to see the dog disappearing in the bushes.

'Come here, you,' he yelled. The dog came cowering and whimpering. 'Come right along.'

He marched back to the swamp-hole, Hank slinking behind. There he turned to the dog, and pointing to the bone, said in a voice of thunder : 'See that ? So it was you all the time. You that was my pard. You that I trusted. Hank, you're a traitor. You're wuss'n a thief ; you're a traitor.'

The dog grovelled at his feet, whined, licked his boot. Jeff spurned him.

'You damned traitor !' Hank raised his big strong head just a little, and howled a very wail of death. He tried to reach his master's feet. The hunter kicked him off, muttering an oath.

'You *traitor* ! Now you come and get what's coming to you !' He strode back to the cabin. Hank slunk far behind in an agony of shame and humiliation.

Garvin took down the ready-loaded rifle, and came out. Hank was grovelling twenty yards away, whining his shame and sorrow.

'Come hyar,' yelled the man. The great hound

214

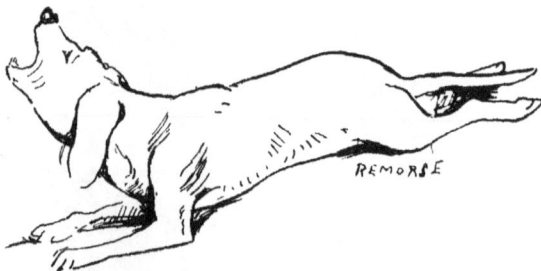

REMORSE

crawled slowly to his very feet, and gazed with blinking eyes on the face he had loved so long and deeply.

Jeff levelled the rifle at his partner's brain, right between the big brown eyes, those bright brave eyes that had ever greeted him in love, that had never yet feared facing death when his master was in peril. And a deep revulsion seized the hunter as he glared.

' No, I won't,' he gasped. ' I can't do it. You are my dawg. But I'm through with you. You played false. I'm through with you.'

He flung himself on his fur-rugged couch, and sobbed like a child.

Inch by inch, the old hound crawled in, slowly, belly to earth. Inch by inch his velvet ears trailed the dust, and his hung lips slobbered on the sill. A little, little moan, he made just one. Slowly he reached the old familiar bear-skin. His master's hand hung down from the bunk.

The dog reached humbly forward, and ventured to lick the hand. At once it was withdrawn, and the hunter sat up. Growling harshly, ' You traitor ! ' he gave the dog a fierce kick. With no sound but the involuntary gasp, the hound crawled out of the door, then raising his muzzle he howled the mournful death-song of a dog that knows he is lost.

Garvin lay in silence for an hour; then glancing at the sun-streak on the floor that was his clock, he rose, took his rifle, slipped a bundle of meat into his wallet, and stepped out. Hank was sprawling with his noble head humiliated in the dust. He raised his big brown eyes, and moaned. He did not raise his head or wag his tail.

'Come on here, you traitor,' said Garvin savagely; and away he marched for two long hours with his humbled partner following far behind.

At last they reached the Ohio River, and the steamboat landing. The *General Jackson* was swinging in to get wood. He had counted on this. The negroes were hard at work, carrying in the cord sticks. On the upper deck were travellers, well-to-do planters and their families. A tall Southerner, leaning on the rail, marked the picturesque group of the skin-clad hunter and the superb dog. He said: 'That's a fine dog you got, my friend.'

'The best b'arhound in all Kentucky,' was the answer.

' Will you sell him ? ' said the planter.

' No,' said the hunter savagely.

' I've taken a fancy to him. I'd give a big price.'

' Not for any price,' was the answer.

' I'd surely love to have him.'

The hunter glared across the river in silence for a time, then abruptly said :

' Would you be good to him ? '

' Yes. I'm a sporting man. I love a good dog. What'll you take for him ? '

' I won't sell him,' growled Garvin with savage finality. ' But—if you'll be good to him, I'll *give* him to you.'

The planter was surprised, but the dog was tied and led up the gang-plank, the leash was placed in the planter's hand, and Garvin returned to the dock.

' My name is La Pine of New Orleans,' said the planter, with an air of one whose name is a guarantee of honourable behaviour.

The steamer swung out. High on the upper deck was Hank near his new master. With his back against a snubbing-post stood Garvin gazing as the open water widening between him and his dog. The old hunter's face writhed in an inner struggle, his eyes were blurred with tears so he could not see much ; but he could hear, and the long agonizing wail that came from that upper deck went through his very soul.

He waved his arm to sign ' Come back '. He shouted, ' Let him go. That's my dawg.' But the steamer sped away.

He turned and travelled now as he seldom had before through the down-stream woods. He knew that twenty miles away was another wooding-dock. The steamer had to make forty miles to reach this point. He spared himself not at all. He covered that rugged twenty miles in little over three hours.

As he came worn and breathless and feebly shouting down the hill, he was just in time to see the *General Jackson* swing away with all the wood she needed.

The river-boys thought him a madman when they heard him. But the familiar explanation ' He missed the boat and got mad about it ' was enough.

' Where do she dock next ? ' was his question when he was calm enough to ask.

' She don't dock till she makes Memphis now,' was all he could find out.

He went back to the cabin, broken-hearted. He tried to think it would blow over in a month or so.

He would get another dog. Then the notion of that was loathsome. 'There ain't no other dawg,' he told himself, and hid his real feeling in mere foul language.

He stuck it out alone for a week. One bright morning, he girded up his thin loins, and set his long hunter legs striding till he came to the trading-store. He had brought what furs he could lay hands on, and everything that promised a little ready money. But his plans were vague.

He sat silently smoking by the open fire till Culberson, the trader, was unoccupied, and sat down at the other side of the hearth.

'Say, Jack,' said Garvin, 'when do the *General Jackson* come back this way?'

'Heh,' said Jack, 'you ain't up to date. She won't come back never.'

'What?'

'Ain't you heard? She struck a sawyer the night after she left here, just below Memphis, and was lost with all aboard. Not a soul saved but the darky cook.'

Garvin stared stupidly. Then in a cold way, he said: 'Wished I'd been aboard her.'

His unspoken purpose had been to go to New

Orleans to seek out his dog, and now the blankness and futility of everything was stupefying.

He had no plans. He could not live his hunter life without his dog, 'and there ain't no other dawg'.

He hated the thought of his desolate shanty. He hung around the ' Corner ' which, with the trading-store, the saloon, and one or two houses, constituted the settlement. After a month, his cash was gone and his credit in danger.

He sat about, gloomily silent, or muttering to himself. The men began to avoid him. He was pointed at as having ' something on his mind—likely killed some one '.

It was in the second month of his loafing that Culberson said : ' Jeff, why don't you take a job ? They want a mail carrier to cover the forty miles between Carrolton and Frankfort.'

Tramping the lonely woods with a mail sack was more to his taste than steady labour. Thus it was that Garvin made the weekly trip, and thus he came to hang around Carrolton docks, and at length to hear much about the sinking of the *General Jackson*.

' No, sah,' said a voice in his hearing. ' They wasn't all drowned. They was one man as had a big dog. That thar dog shur toted 'im ashore.'

220

'What did you call him ? '

'Pine or Lavine or something like that.'

'And went on to New Orleans ? ' said Garvin, with interest that almost scared the negro.

'Ah don' know. Ah 'spose so.'

He went as a deck hand, but in two weeks Garvin was in New Orleans. The name La Pine was slowly sufficient. He stood at last in a big house, to be kindly received by the tall planter.

'Where is my dawg ? ' was the blunt and passionate opening.

Then he heard a simple tale. The sinking of the *General Jackson* was all too true. Every passenger but one was lost. La Pine's big dog had safely borne him down the midnight flood to a friendly shore.

Arrived in New Orleans, he was made much of by the children, and responded to their friendship. But many times they missed him, and found him again down by the docks, watching some steamer coming in, watching and sniffing at every man who came down the gang-plank ; or howling as it sped away.

Two months went by. Hank was an established

member of the family, loved by the children. Had he not rescued their father from death ?

And less often now, he went to the dock-front to wail.

But one day, a hamper arrived from a friend in the hills. When opened, it disclosed six smoked bear hams.

Hank entered the room as they were being displayed. He sniffed intensely, gave a short yelp and dashed out and away. On the lawn, he stopped and howled a heart-rending howl, then ran. When last they saw him, he was running like mad toward the dock.

La Pine mounted horse, and followed. He was too late to see it, but many witnesses there were.

' That big houn' dawg jes lep in the water when he seen that there steamer. Them men in that boat tried to pull him out, but he bit at them. He jes was plumb bound he'd swim under that steamboat, an' the paddles struck him and dar he is.'

Yes, there he was, crushed, still warm, with battered body and a broken skull.

Pointing to a spot under the cypress trees, La Pine continued : ' That's where he lies. We all loved him.'

222

The hunter stared his wild animal stare. Slowly his words were rasped out :

' He—were—mah—dawg—I didn't—oughter—done—it. I had oughter forguv him—like he would me. He were mah dawg. He—were—mah—dawg.'

He turned and was lost sight of.

There is a little white stone in a place of honour under the cypresses and moss of New Orleans. Six months later, there was an unnamed, now-forgotten, mound two thousand miles away on the track of the Forty-niners. But no one knows that their histories were closely bound together. They are the graves of Hank and Jeff.

XVI

La Bête, the Beast Wolf of Gevaudan

I

NEXT after Courtaud of the Paris siege, as an historic figure of surpassing magnitude in the animal world, was the awful beast wolf of Gevaudan. A fearsome giant of the race was the beast, La Bête de Gevaudan, le Loup Garou, the giant wolf; for by all of these names was he known, though most in story as La Bête.

When, after three years of bloody feud with man, he fell, fighting an army of nearly fifty thousand hunters, he was found to be, not a demon, horned and hoofed, but an ordinary wolf of gigantic size, three feet at the shoulder, taller than any mastiff or Great Dane, and above all equipped with jaws that rivalled those of lion or hyene.

Little light is there on his early history. What

there is might be called myth or surmise. Ther
is a story told by a hunter, a *braconnier*, Pierr
Cuellac, of Lodève in Mercoire, that he by lon
craft and careful tracking had found the den of
mother wolf ; and yet, strange to relate, herei
not one but two mother wolves had joined thei
homes and their broods. The females fled at h
approach, for he came with hounds and with arme
men ; and he, Pierre, the bravest of them al
crawled into the rocky ledge, and there shiverin
before him, or in some cases growling defianc
he found no less than twelve wolf cubs, a doubl
brood. Mindful of the bounty on every wolf, h
slew them, one by one, except the last. That on
was a little larger, and a little darker, and a littl
more defiant than the rest.

Cuellac was held for a moment by the old foreste
tradition : ' Thou shalt not take all the eggs ; tho
shalt not kill all the brood ; leave some for seed o
comfort.' And, as he halted in his bloody worl
he saw in the farthest corner—yes, he swears it-
that this, the last fell pup of an ill-born race, di
raise his right forepaw, and on his black and impis
visage made the true sign of the Cross. Th
torches flared a little brighter, and gave a perfe

226

view. Cuellac swears it ; and whether the pious
act meant devil or devotee, he bowed to the holy
sign and backed him from the cave, with eleven
dead wolflings dangling from his hands.

Thus one, the choicest of the double brood, was
left ; and, having two fond dams to feed and foster,
he grew as never wolf had grown before. Three
years later—so the forest folk believe—he came
forth as Loup Garou, La Bête, a giant demon with
a charmed life, the dreaded Loup de Cevennes, the
Loup Garou with a mission of revenge, vengeance
for the death of his brothers, the avenger of mother
and foster-mother ; ten human lives, it seemed, was
his demand for every single kinsman that they slew.

2

It was in the spring of 1763. Old Cuellac, the
shepherd, father of Cuellac the *braconnier* of Mercoire Forest, who raided the wolf den, was herding
his sheep on this side Ardèche where its lush pas-
tures slope to the lordly Rhone. They were indeed
the very sheep that the family had bought with the
blood-gold, the bounty paid for each of the
slaughtered cubs that long-gone day.

Among his kind, old Cuellac was accounted wealthy, for the bounty cash was ten livres for a scalp ; and eleven times ten being one hundred and ten, would buy some fifty-five sheep, which in these three years gone, had multiplied to one hundred ewes, though table toll was weekly taken by the family of their owner.

And Cuellac *père*, reclining on a bank with his trusty sheep dog, found pleasure in noting the bulging bellies of the ewes, the promise of a new engenderment.

He was chewing the root of a calamus, or water-weed, for these folk knew not the solace of a pipe. He had taken off a sabot to shake it free of pebbles from the outer world, when a growl of alarm from black Fidel set him agape ; and the sudden scurrying and bleating of the sheep completed a scene of terror ; for there among and around the helpless bleaters were two grim wolves, one of enormous size, the other less. They were slaughtering sheep even as a man with a club might slaughter rabbits in a pen, when at them, valiant in his righteousness, dashed brave Fidel.

It was the work of a moment for these two great monsters to seize the poor devoted dog, and rend

228

him body and limb. Then on the sheep they sprang again ; but Cuellac went racing to the spot, and with his iron-bound shepherd's staff he smote both right and left at the circling raiders. They turned on him. With his back against a rock, he faced them ; and he slashed and thrust and yelled the shepherd cry for help : '*Aux secours ! Aux secours ! Le Loup ! Le Loup !* '

But his arm was weakening. Many a blow that missed robbed him of power ; and, though he heard afar and nearer a hunter in response, '*Venons ! Venons !* ' the wolves closed in ; old Cuellac was downed. His throat and body were protected with his goatskin kirtle ; but he was down on his face, partly under a rock, the grim wolf chopping, tearing the flesh from his thighs and legs, as the hunter horn was heard, and a burst of belling from the wolfhounds. Then the two grim wolves pricked up their ears, wheeled, passed from view like drifting storms of dust.

A moment later, the hounds with the huntsmen arrived. Young Cuellac it was, and what a scene ! A dozen sheep were dead, a score at least were wounded, and others stampeding in stupid terror ; while, here in the centre of the group was staunch

Fidel, dead—stone dead ; and old man Cuellac soon to follow on the same dark trail.

His son raised him a little, gave him wine from a hunter's flask, and in faltering accents the old man told the tale : ' A giant wolf ! A three-times wolf, *mon Dieu !* Dark, very dark of front, and three light bars like streaks of sunlight on his ribs ! A monster ! A Loup Garou ! *Mon Dieu !* Water ! Water ! Help me, Sainte Vièrge ! *Mon Dieu ! Mes Moutons ! Sacré—parbleu ! Mon fils ! Oh-h ! Dieu ! '*

And old Cuellac was dead.

This was La Bête's first fell attack on man, so far as known. But others in the near past were now charged against him. And this much is certain : on this very day it was that the brute learned man-meat was good, and thenceforth the dread beast of Gevaudan a man-eater became.

3

The very next day, without delay, the country-side assembled for a fight ' to the death ' they said. Vows of vengeance from near relatives, wild an-

nouncements from irresponsibles, and the public
notification by the Seigneur de Florac that double
bounty would be paid for the scalp of La Bête—
twenty livres, a fortune surely in itself.

There were houndsmen and hunters there as good
as Pierre Cuellac, but it seemed the right and proper
thing to make him captain of this hunt.

To the very spot they went where the tragedy
had taken place. The rabble was cautioned to hold
back while Pierre with three or four good men,
louvetiers who knew the hounds, went forward on
the trail of yesterday.

Before they had gone two miles, they crossed a
swampy place ; and in the mud read this : that
two wolves had been there the day before—one a
big strong giant wolf with paws like a bear's ; the
other much smaller, probably a female, for they ran
in pairs, and the small one dragged a crippled limb.
How this did hearten men and dogs !

The bugle sounded the fanfare that meant ' Come
on ! ' and the waiting rabble at the rendezvous
responded with a cheer.

The going had been slow, for the scent was cold.
But the hunters followed the *limiers*, the fine old
bloodhounds with the marvellous noses, and were

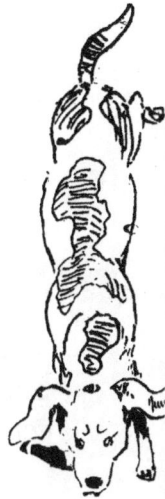

231

led ever faster till they reached a basking-place where the wolves must have tarried for hours. After that, the scent was good and the pace grew hot.

It was nigh the nooning when amidst the roar augmenting, a new loud note—a trumpet note—*ta-ra-ra-ra*, announced to all the world that the quarry was in view—the wolves, a giant and a lesser grey—the very same of yesterday's tragedy.

Then there was a marvellously short run, when the yelping of the hounds and later the huntsman's horn announced that the quarry was at bay. Where? How? What?

The wiser hunters went ahead, and learned the truth. The chase was short because the lesser wolf was too crippled to run, and the big one would not leave her.

The grim bandits had chosen a good place for the final stand—between two rocks in a tangled thicket. The dogs were all around; but the big wolf faced the front way and the lesser wolf the back.

There was much loud mouthing from the dogs, but nary one would venture in. Those jaws meant certain death to the first at least.

Now did Cuellac crawl up between the dogs. With him were men that carried bows and arrows, some flintlocks, and one a short thick blunderbuss. But to use these now would more likely hurt the dogs than the wolves. So Cuellac crawled around behind, hoping for a higher stand. He got a good look at the lesser wolf, fighting bravely on three legs. He climbed to a higher rock, called for a bow, and at short range from up above, he pierced her through and through. Her scream of pain brought great Garou to her side; he drew the arrow with his teeth, then laid about among the dogs.

The huntsman yelled: 'Charge, or we lose every dog !' The rabble closed with yells, with spears and blasts of powder and of horn. They closed in from the front. The one way open was the back ; so the great wolf sprang over the corpses of his foes and of his loved one, and away—unwounded, quite unharmed, his courage unshaken, but his wild fierce soul aflame with hate, a-craze for soon revenge.

233

4

The hunters crowded around, helped this and that big hound with bandage or with lotion-balm. Not a few were dead, gashed dead by the great jaws; and at the farther end, the body of his mate, a she-wolf, that had elsewhere looked a monster, but seen as she was by Garou's side, seemed small.

The arrow had pierced her vitals. The crippled leg was surely the work of old Cuellac's shepherd crook.

'Yes,' said Pierre Cuellac, 'I am sure it is the same. This grim brute that killed my father is the dark-visaged cub that, in that den three years ago, forfended death, made me hold back by his cursed use of the blessed sign—a demon wolf, a Loup Garou. I felt it then! I know it now! But, by the blessed sign that he profaned, I swear I will never quit! I will follow, follow, while my strength holds out, till he or I lie low.'

It was not late in the day, but the rabble had no further stomach for the fray; and, bearing as a little triumph, the body of the she-Garou, they scattered homeward, some to vow they sought no more such hunting, some to plan protection for

234

their herds ; he, Cuellac, to prepare for a new hard
hunt with better weapons, fiercer dogs, and priestly
bans and amulets with which to fight the demon
wolf, uncharm the charm which guarded Loup
Garou.

5

Meanwhile Loup Garou went galloping, galloping, galloping, over moor and timberland, listening
without fear for the yelling pack that might be
following. But they came not ; they had paid
heavy toll for their little victory. Nor dog nor
man minded then for further adventuring.

Little is known of his line of travel, but this much
later was divined from sundry tracks and glimpses
of the beast : he had reached the environs of the
little parish of Marvejols ; and, though he surely
must have been hungry, he passed some sheep,
some calves—all easy prey—and, overleaping a
fence, confronted the fat little Curé Murat, who,
with his dog, was homeward wending, with
pleasant thoughts of dinner in his mind. The
dog had time for half a dozen barks—that was
all. And, having stilled the spaniel, the great wolf

seized the Curé by the throat, and tore his life out.

Then, calmly it would seem, he lay like a lion on his prey, tore off the clerical husks, and feasted on the warm and quivering human meat, licked the blood and feasted, and worked it with his tongue for freer bleeding, till it grew stiff, till his belly bulged. Then silently he leaped the hedge, and headed far away.

It was dark before the anxious servants of the Curé found the mangled form. It was not for two days after that the expert hunters succeeded in piecing together the glimpses, the facts, the witness : a giant wolf, black-visaged ; and another said : ' Yes, with three pale bars across his ribs.' And then it was surely known that this was the work of Loup Garou, the Gevaudan man-eating wolf.

6

A wave of terror had followed the news of Cuellac's tragic death. It was succeeded by a wave of horror when the Curé was added to the list. Some said it proved that the wolf was a devil incarnate ; and some that it proved the opposite, for the good Curé was in his canonicals, protected by crucifix and all.

This was the sum-total of result : the church added to the bounty fund, thirty livres was offered for the head of La Bête. And news of a mighty hunt was spread. Several of the nobles brought their retainers and their hounds. The whole parish of Marvejols was enlisted, and the country scoured for many miles. But never a sign found they of Loup Garou.

A month went by with spasmodic efforts. A little wolf was indeed killed ; but all that could be shown was that the giant wolf had disappeared from the earth ; and comfort in the thought that this was more than flesh and blood ; it was a demon, a werwolf, a Loup Garou indeed.

The summer waned with little loss by wolves. But in the later harvest-time, news—shocking news—was brought. A giant wolf, the very same, had raided a field of harvesters near Le Vegin, had massacred them, had feasted, and had disappeared like a cursed thing that came and went without a trace.

Another futile hunt was organized, and nothing

achieved—little proved indeed except this—that the man-eater's habit was to kill, then fly some fifty or sixty miles away, then repeat his adventure and leave another village in tears.

So passed the autumn and the early winter. It was definitely known now that La Bête was a confirmed man-eater ; that he had killed and feasted on a dozen human beings, and never returned to his kill.

The winter deepened, that hard white winter of 1764. There appeared more wolves, far more than usual, for deep snow in the mountains was driving them down. Les Vosges as well as the High Cevennes contributed ravening packs that harried sheep, and even killed shepherds ; but when the shepherd was actually devoured and the sheep untouched, it was known for the work of La Bête.

7

At this time, there was at Nîmes a famous heiress. Her father had been a merchant prince at Marseilles. His ships had sailed the Seven Seas with marvellous success. His silk factories had poured gold into his coffers. His factories had been at Marseilles, but his château, his estates, and his home of leisure had been at Nîmes.

He had been accounted the richest man of the South ; and it was rumoured that in return for help in the Dutch War, the King had been about to confer a patent of nobility on the shrewd Provençal. At the moment of his best success, he had been stricken with a fatal illness. He passed away, leaving all his vast possessions to his only child, the beautiful Yvonne.

She had a dozen worshippers among the young men of the time and of the Court. She was, indeed, the Belle of Provence, for she was charming as well as wise and beautiful. But still she was heart-free.

Gallant young fellows were the nobles that paid her court ; and, as they flocked around her at the great ball, she was gracious to all. But, clamouring for some kindly favour, she announced with a merry laugh : ' I could love a little, perhaps in time could even marry, the man who will bring me the head of La Bête. But it must be himself that takes it —not a huntsman, not a mob of hirelings.'

That is why young gallant Roussillon pushed

forward, dropped on one knee, and, with hand on heart, and fervent voice, exclaimed :

' Oh, lovely princess ! I claim the right of first attempt. At dawn, I go forth, and will never come back till I bring the monster's head.'

A very proper young man was the Seigneur de Roussillon, of high degree, well trained in arms and *vénerie*, brave as a lion, a model knight of chivalry.

At dawn he was away, mounted, and attended by mounted men, and a pack of his own staunch hounds. He was bound to meet the giant wolf, single-handed ; but his vow did not prevent his having help to find the foe. And many a league they rode from Nîmes northerly and westerly, till they reached the rocky foothills of the High Cevennes, whence latest tidings had reached them of the awful Loup Garou.

Yes, at the little village of Tarn on this side Florac, they confirmed the rumour. La Bête had come, had killed, had feasted his ghoulish feast, and gone—a week ago.

There are clever *braconniers* in Lozère—semi-out-laws, but deep in wisdom of the woods. For the most part, they mask their poaching lives as char-coal-burners. It was to these that Roussillon addressed himself. A present reward for information, to be trebled if it be proven true !

So he learned the little that they knew : the great wolf had come to them from the south, and would not likely go that way now again. He would not go west to Espelion, for it was open plains there ; nor northerly to Marvejols, for there they were organized to meet him. So that most surely he went easterly through the High Cevennes to Ardèche. That was all any one knew, and that was mere surmise.

Thus it was that, in spite of winter weather and leagues of heavy trail, young Roussillon pressed on with but a rumour for his guide. Within a week, he had visited every village in Ardèche, seeking for news.

Then came a courier with the word he craved. The giant wolf had made a kill near Yssingeaux in the Haute-Loire. It was fifty miles to the north, through a land of rugged rocks and tangled forests. But he and his train set out, and within forty-eight hours were on the spot.

They found the weeping family, the mangled shepherd ; but that was two days back. Where was the monster now ?

There had been a little snow in the woods, so the hunters were able to follow the tracks whose scent was cold. They followed all day, most of the time on foot ; and when night came, they had crossed the wooded hills, and were now near Tournon on the Rhone.

Here they bivouacked ; and on the morn took the trail again. Then for the first time, the *limiers*, the bloodhounds, owned the scent, and led the chase.

Ten miles brought them to the brimming Rhone, and every proof that they could find told this : the giant wolf had sprung in, had faced the icy flood, and crossed into Le Drôme. There was no bridge at all, but boats were found. The hounds were embarked and ferried over, while gallant Roussillon rode and guided his own horse as it swam across the winter flood.

The trail was found again, the hounds gave valiant tongue, and on went all.

Due east of Valence is the little town of Die, nestling in the foothills of the mountain spur that forms the western edge of the Hautes-Alpes. Die is a town of shepherds and of farmers ; the pine forests cover all the mountains to the east.

Here they found in larger measure than they hoped the very news they sought. A great wolf had been seen in broad daylight. His head was very dark, and three buff bars were angled on his ribs. Rejoicing, they hastened to the spot. They found the trail, red-hot; and away the joyous hunting, hopeful crew, across the Grand Pré, up a small river valley, and into an open field where sheep were huddled in a far-fenced fold.

The dogs led fast across, but in a moment roared a full-voiced roar, and then hung back, formed a circle, raised their muzzles, and raved to the skies. The hunters came as quickly as might be, to find the dogs were grouped around—a corpse, a shepherd, face-down, wallowed in red blood, torn, twisted, and the flesh from his throat and neck devoured.

Men from the near farmhouses were seen running, shouting as they came. All gathered around the horror. The tracks, the every detail told the tale—that this was Garou's latest kill.

8

Now had the gods given all the hunters asked —a chance, a final match, a valiant show-down each to each. The hounds went on the trail at highest speed, the hunters galloped after.

Then came a local hunter with the offer of his help. He knew the hills, and when the hounds led into a rocky glen on this side of Montegriffe, the Alpman cried : ' You've got him now ! There is no way ahead for his escape ! '

The huntsmen cheered, the horn sent notes of triumph, the hounds gave noble tongue.

' But here,' said valiant Roussillon, ' is where I go alone.'

So he ranged his fellows all around the glen, at every point where it seemed possible to scale the rocks. The bloodhounds were called off—their part was done. Only a brace of fighting lurchers went in with the brave young knight. He sought a single-handed fight, armed only with his sword, but he needed the dogs to find the foe.

As silent as may be he followed in, his sword in hand, his every sense alert. The two brave dogs went forward, sniffing the track, and watching every bush. So, in a fearsome silence, they were lost to view.

A half-hour passed in eerie calm. Then there was a fierce outburst of war-dog song, a human

shout, another, a yelp, a wailing cry—and a silence
stony dead.

The hunters, manning all the rocks around, kept
still and held their stand for half an hour as they had
been enjoined. Then all closed in.

The centre of the glen they reached, and here they
found young Roussillon dead and dabbling in his
blood, his throat torn out ; and near on either side,
the fighting dogs, both dead and disembowelled.

But the wolf ! Where was he ? Gone, and not
a trace of him that any one could see or any hound
would own.

The tracks and gory splashes told the tale. The
dread Garou had craftily doubled back, climbed and
crouched on a high rock overlooking his own trail ;
and, as the gallant knight came stealthily by, the
wolf had leaped upon him from above and behind,
had spilled his life at a chop, then easily dispatched
the dogs. And now was gone. Where ? The
hunters never knew, nor was he seen again for
weeks, so it was said, until his red, red trail was
found again at Rourke in far Auvergne, one
hundred miles away.

That was the end of gallant Roussillon ; and that
was the end of all attempts to meet the demon

single-handed. Weekly accounts came to blazon
in ever more lurid announcement the horrid progress of the man-eater. Men, women, and children
were furnishing his daily food ; since that tragic
day by Mercoire Forest in the June of 1763, he had
killed and devoured not less than eighty human
beings, and scoffed at all attempts to destroy him
from the land.

9

The New Year dawned with little New Year's
joy in rugged Gevaudan. The grim wolf stalked
across the land, a form of death, invulnerable
himself, and all his trail was red with human blood.

Then did the good Bishop of Mende, recognizing
the magnitude of the calamity that was upon them,
call for a day of special public prayer in the
Cathedral of Mende on 7 February, 1765.

Leaders of people were there, and no pirate that
ever descended on their coasts received more dread
attention than that wolf. The bounty set upon the
demon's head was doubled and redoubled, and the
State of Languedoc offered a tenfold price—2,400
livres for his life.

The energetic old Bishop made a special trip to
Paris to interest the King, and enlist his royal help.
Louis XV was busy—with his pleasures chiefly ;
but he gave audience to the Bishop, and sent a
contribution of 6,000 livres to be added to the
bounty fund.

Ten thousand livres it was now in total. Many
a famous man has been hunted down for a tenth of
that.

Then, urged, inspired and cheered on by the good
Bishop, a mighty hunt was organized. Choosing
the central region of Languedoc where last the
monster had been known to range, every man in it
who was capable of bearing arms was commanded
to appear in hunting-gear on the 7th of March,
1765, at the nearest given point. Some fifty of
these points were named ; so that on that grim,
forbidding winter morn the region of the wolf
was surrounded with a necklace of hostile camps,
besides unnumbered dogs, making an army of 20,000
men, all armed to the teeth, and consecrating their
every effort to the task of killing the terrible wolf.

The region enclosed was about twenty miles
across, which meant that when the men were
spread, they were about seven yards apart—or

would have been—but no man cared to be alone when the beast should come. So that there were gaps of twenty or thirty yards at first, but these grew rapidly less; and late in the evening, when the ring was but a couple of miles across, the great wolf appeared like a flash. He, as ever, sprang without warning from behind a thick cover, killed his man, threw down another, and would have finished him but a peasant with a mattock brought down his weapon on the monster's head, inflicting a glancing wound; whereat the grim wolf sprang on him, gashed him with a lightning chop, then bounded off beyond the ring to be lost in the gloom —lost—gone—the great hunt ended in a total failure.

There were clamorous critical murmurs among the hunters. They realized now that they were a rabble of farmers, aided by cur-dogs. What they lacked was trailing bloodhounds and fighting wolf-hounds. Also they were not led by expert hunters of the wolf.

Spurred on by the fighting Bishop, they canvassed all the near-by châteaux for the best support, with some slight filling of their needs. The men kept on; they felt they must, for a slight fall of snow on the ground offered a rare chance to follow and find, however cold the scent.

The men were two days in getting placed, and again made a huge surround. Then the track of the great wolf was found, recognized by the size ; and when the place where he had crouched was seen, the hunters rejoiced, for the snow where his head had lain was stained with a deep red stain.

There could be no doubt that the blow was a trifling and far from disabling wound. And yet the discomfort of it had prevented the great wolf going, as had been his wont, far, far away from the scene of each new kill.

Again the tactics of the last surround were used. The drive was made complete ; the big track was seen again and again. And then it was wholly lost, and never more seen by any hunter of that hunt nor any clue to how it disappeared. Some there were who claimed that this demon could at will go on and leave no track, like sorcerers who can omit their shadow if they please. But the hunter who best knew such things believed that the monster, crafty as he was cruel, had waded for a mile down some unfrozen brook, and so given all the slip.

This much is known : he next was heard of fifty

miles away, and now was killing not once or twice a week, but every day, a fearful human massacre. As the tale of horror spread, the chance for great renown increased. Famous hunters came, from Provence, and Languedoc, Vivarac, Comtat, Dauphine, and up among the Alpes whose hunters claim to rank above the world. They came to try their luck ; but when they came in numbers, they never saw him ; when they tried it single-handed, they left their bones for lesser wolves to pick.

The terror grew.

Not less than one hundred and twenty persons he had killed and feasted on. The peasantry along the forest-edge moved out ; all solitary houses were abandoned, and terror-driven folk were massing in the high-walled towns, so that the farms were deserted throughout low Gevaudan, and famine threatened all. The great Rhone Valley, fifty by one hundred miles, was in terror, was being deserted as fast as folk could go.

10

Again the good old Bishop Mende set out for Paris, there to see the King.

Many stories of the terror reign had reached him, and had lost nothing in the telling, so now he was in mood to listen.

There was a dash of romance in Louis XV. The sad narrative stirred him; it sounded like the ancient heroic wars with dragons. He was not easily moved to action; but when he was, he generally set other men and other things a-moving too.

'Without doubt,' said he to the Bishop, 'this dire calamity has come upon you for some great sin the people have committed, possibly sacrilege—more likely disloyalty to the Crown, in thought if not in deed—which really is treason, than which no sin is more abhorrent in the sight of God. Therefore, we set aside a special day of penance for the sin, and of High Mass and prayers in all the churches for delivery from this brute. Let us say July twenty-first.

'Next, we will order a vast, a national hunt, to run the Hell-hound down. Next, we will put in charge our beloved Marquis of Enneval, the most famous of our nobles who hunt wolves; he who extirpated the black wolves of Brétagne, and slew when all else failed the grim grey Wolf of Soissons.

A thousand wolves have fallen before his prowess and his hounds. Him without doubt we send with sureness of success.

' Every *seigneur* of lands within a hundred leagues must join with all his hunters and his hounds. Every peasant within twenty miles must come with his weapons and his dogs.

' We will send our whole standing army to give them orderly approach, and staunch support; and to fully play on every human motive, we will double the bounty fund. Fifteen thousand livres, you say it is ? By our royal word, we will make it thirty thousand livres, to be divided according to rank among those who are in at the death.'

This in brief was the plan and promise of the King ; and thus was set a-going the most tremendous hunt the world has ever known on the trail of a single wild beast.

II

These were the events which led up to the great hunt of Gevaudan. On that famous 1st of August, 1765, they met, not all at one place, but at half a dozen appointed places covering the middle valley of the Rhone, from Avignon to St. Étienne, from Isère down to Gard—a hundred miles each way, for this was Garou's range, and no one knew just where or when to find the fiend.

And these were the hunters assembled : the gallant riding Marquis of Enneval, the killer of a thousand wolves, no longer young, but wise in leadership ; his cousin, Seigneur Antoine, the most expert swordsman in France, with Puy de Dôme, Allier, L'Isère and Hérault ; hunters all and men of fame. And last, the Captain Reinhard, keeper of the King's own wolfhounds, with three hundred seasoned hounds, each as heavy as a common wolf, and known to the world to-day as Great Danes. Three hundred of the rough swift greyhounds known as northern wolfhounds, all much swifter than the swiftest wolf.

Two hundred *limiers*, that is, fine-bred bloodhounds that can follow with certainty a trail though it be three days old. Many packs of various hounds brought by the nobles and the hunters of the stricken range ; and last as rabble, following these, the sheep-dogs, bull-dogs, and bandogs, mongrels, and escapes of the peasant homes, that swelled the list a full 2,000 more.

The King had sent his whole standing army—
only 10,000 men, but soldiers, trained to follow
without fear, and do as ordered and not come back
until their task was done.

Joining with the nobles were hunters from the
hills, farmers, retainers and peasants—not less than
23,000 men.

With this vast concourse, we must also reckon
horses and wagons that drew the needed supplies,
and the good old sporting Bishop Mende prancing
around on his mule, exhorting, praying, directing.

Now, what a picture on the bright calm day on
the shimmering Rhone—that famous first day of
August, 1765. There were assembled 43,000 armed
men, and not less than 4,000 dogs, to go after one
big solitary wolf, sworn to follow till they got him.
One might think that a simple feat, with such
support.

They failed and failed and failed.

12

Under the guidance of the great Marquis, they
all set forth at dawn. Bugles and hunt-horns
shrilled the messages ; mounted couriers rode with

orders here and there ; beacon fires on distant hills were blazing.

A great cordon drive had been planned to begin in the High Cevennes, and work southward in a crescent toward the men one hundred miles away.

Many little mishaps there were those first few days ; and common wolves were seen, but none were killed. The killing was to mark the end.

On the fifth day, as the wings had been ordered to swing together, a messenger came on a foam-splashed horse, shouting : ' You haven't got him in there at all ; he's back here and has just killed the Abbé le Puy.'

There was nothing for it but to face about, spread out, sweep northward toward the mountains, and tramp, tramp, tramp.

Again after three days, just as they seemed to find good signs, another messenger came riding like death on a white horse : ' He isn't here ! He's off in Drôme, and has just wiped out the whole Montelimart family.'

Again they had to face about, spread out, and tramp, tramp, tramp, day after day, week after week. Yes, almost month after month it was.

The men were worn out with endless marching,

with insufficient food and sleep. But their orders were to stay with him till they got him. And on they went in dogged weariness, tramp, tramp, tramp.

For seven long weeks, that hunt went on, tramp, tramp, tramp. Then, on that thrilling day, September 18th, the bugles and the beacon fires spread the joyful news that at last, the surround—the fifteenth surround—was complete, and the great wolf had been seen within.

A surround for him did not mean a man here and another ten feet away. The men had to be shoulder to shoulder, with pikes on guard, and three men deep, or they could not face him. Much of superstitious terror there was in this no doubt to unnerve the men ; and yet he had the prowess to inspire fell fear. He never failed to use a chance. It is claimed that in those long hard weeks he had picked off a dozen of the men who were out to get him. Thus he lived on the enemy, and was undismayed.

But now they surely had him. He was seen again and again—a giant wolf, black-faced, with three buff bars across his ribs. For two more days they followed.

Then, on the twentieth of the month, the cordon, triumphant, bloodathirst, closed in and in, till the armed men were ten deep all around him. Still it was a vast ring, and the baying of the bandogs set the mountains and the welkin all a-ring with rolling clamoration gone joy-mad.

Many lesser wolves had fallen, and the long, long hunt seemed finishing in grand battle. But still the giant was in power, and raging, waging bitter war.

The ring grew smaller yet. In the final wooded stretch, the beast was brought to bay ; his towering form sufficient mark.

Then the bugles and the hunt-horns blew, blew the *arrêt—Ta-ra ta-ra ta-ra ta-ta-ta !* Hold, hold ! Silence, all stand ! Silent, stand !

The men held still ; the dogs were hard to hold. But in the semi-silence following the blast, the leader Enneval cried out, and his herald counterparted after him :

> ' *The hour of gloire is come !*
> *The great beast is at bay !*
> *He is crouching in yon wood,*
> *The desolator of a hundred homes !*

The beast that ne'er knew mercy or defeat !
He is ready for his last outrance !
Who will face him ?
For Beast and Fiend combined is he !
Who values gloire above his life ?
Who here is ready for the death ? '

And many valiant men there were—too many—
who were ready for the brunt. So great Enneval
waved his hand and pointed to Antoine and Reinhard and Aubusson and half a dozen more of mettle
tried. Most were gentlefolk, but one stood forth
with blazing eye, a peasant with a proud man's soul,
and cried :

' My lord, I crave a placement in the line ! I,
Cuellac of Lodève ! I knew him at the first ; I
would meet him at the last. He killed my father.
I would face him to the death—my father's soul and
mine, my lord ! I have a mandate from the Lord
of Battles and of Beasts. I pray you send me in ! '

So the chosen band fared forth into the final
wood. All ahead, and left and right, was roaring
with the blare of horns, and hounds held back ;
but very silent was the onset of the stalwart ten.

Misguided by the silence, the wolves in this last
glorious stand moved toward the chosen men. A

small wolf and another issued forth with flash of
fur and flash of teeth, and falchion flash to meet
them.

A dozen were forced out, and fighting, fell.
Then, after a time of truce between, a larger bulk
loomed in the shady copse.

'Look out! *En garde!* He comes!' And
brasting forth, the Ajax of his race, the great wolf
loomed, misled by silence in the chosen band, he
dashed at them.

'*En garde! En garde!*' and every man stood
braced as though to face the onset of a bull.

Reinhard was armed with a cannon blunderbuss,
the broad stock firm against his shoulder braced.
He fired a raking volley in the wolf's right flank.
. It stung the wolf, but the back shock downed the
man. The wolf was on him in a flash, and slashed
and did him death. But Cuellac with his boar
spear, sprang between. Thanks to the impact of
his mighty frame, the wolf impaled himself, yet
threw back Cuellac on the prostrate Reinhard's
writhing form, and slashed his arm, his head, his
neck, and spilled his life; while Enneval, Antoine,
and Aubusson closed in with falchions drawn and
pierced him through and through.

So the great wolf fell, slashing, fighting, dead ;
defiant, grinding the iron spear in his teeth,
triumphant, dead—dead upon the pile of those that
he had slain ; dead, yes ! but still triumphant ; he
was dead.

XVII

Courtaud, The King Wolf of France

This is the story of Great Courtaud, the king wolf; the wolf that ruled all Central France like a ferocious despotic monarch; the wolf that drove a thousand men in flight before him; the wolf that shut up all Paris in a state of siege for three hard years of snow; the wolf that sent King Charles into poltroon hiding behind his castle walls of stone; the wolf that every day devoured a man as a dog might maul his daily ration bone.

I

THE hand of God was heavy laid on France those days. Armies from England were devastating all Normandy in their senseless fury of destruction; Burgundy, Brittany, Luxembourg, and Provence were under their own warlords in conflict with the central kingdom ; anarchy, starvation, and disease were raging and rampant in the land ; the helpless peasantry were slaughtered like rabbits ; and the rich farmlands were let run waste.

At such a time it was that the pirate bands of ravening wolves, no longer held in check by hunters of heroic force and high emprise, swept from the woods across the desolated fields, and raided towns and hamlets even as the wolfish human pirates did. In all the lowlands of the Loire, the sheep were gone—devoured, destroyed. The cattle that were left were herded by peasants and defended with such weapons as were at hand. By night, they were safe corralled in barns or high stockades.

But ever the number dwindled, and the packs of hungry wolves grew bigger and bolder. Each village had its skift of wolves that lurked all day in wait for stragglers—men or kine—or boldly came by night to scour the streets.

Paris, the royal city of the Seine, was in those days wholly on 'the island', moated by the Seine on every side, guarded by walls of stone. Paris was the biggest market in all France ; and to Paris were driven small herds of cattle every day. They

vere under guard of armed men, but hungry
volves had little fear of men those times. The
rampling and bellowing of a herd of beeves was
imply a summons to a feast.

Because more cattle came to Paris than to any
ther mart, there were more wolves gathered
long the way to profit by the abundant food.
)ther circumstances helped the wolves. On the
orth bank of the river, just west of the road that
eached the bridge from the north, was a rugged
len, a wilderness of cavernous rocks, disguised
nd hidden in a boscage of brambles, vines and
oppice growth. It had no large trees; all of
hese had long ago been cut for city use as fuel.
3ut the new-grown jungle, combined with the
abyrinthine caves, made a veritable wolf strong-
old that dogs dared not enter, horsemen could
ot enter, and hunters were so handicapped that
he place was abandoned and notorious as the
onvrier or Remise des Loups.

Here it was known that many wolves had their
lens, and each year new litters of cubs were born,
o be a terror on the roads that led to the great
:ity. It was many generations before the place
vas cleaned up; and the only memory of its

savage denizens left to-day is the name, the same
but shortened, that attaches to the place—the
Louvre.

But in the dreadful days of Charles VII, the great
wolf den was in its prime, and yearly sent forth
hungry packs whose right to feast on the royal
herds was the right of major might.

Stretching from the Seine northward to Montmartre, and many leagues to east and west, was the
same wild waste of scrubby oak and vine-entangled
swamps. Winding through these were the three
great thoroughfares that served the folk when
business brought them to the town ; and in
these harbouring jungle tracts, there prowled and
swarmed the wolves.

2

In spring and early summer the wolves are
seldom in packs ; the pair are attending to their
young, now in the dens. But when, in September,
their young go forth to learn the world, and when
still later, the search for food becomes acute, the
packs are formed. In the hardest stress of weather,
with snow upon the ground, the packs grow great,

id sweep the country for their prey with terrible
estructive power.

By the natural law of selection, these packs had
ich a leader, one distinguished above the others
'r his size, his strength, and his sagacity. Many
these leaders were known, were only too well
10wn, to the herdsmen and the city dwellers
ho might meet the ravening packs when business
•rced the men to quit the sheltering walls and
urney through the woods. There was the
lack Wolf of Soissons ; the Red Wolf who had
lled the Seigneur d'Arlu ; the Silver Beast,
i Bête Argentée, known by his silvery-grey
ilour, and notorious for having single-handed
vercome and slain three armed men who sought
• drive him from a valued colt.

But the most terrible of all these hero wolves
as the great grim monster, later known by his
storic name Courtaud.

Born he was—so say the monkish chroniclers—
the wild glen fastness that was known this side
e river northward and westward of the Paris
itering bridge. Here in Le Louvrier, he and his
ate and his kind found safety and retreat.

There can be little doubt that he was born in

265

1424, for he first appeared in full stature and development in the summer of 1427. He w readily distinguished afar by his magnificent si and bearing, for he was a giant among wolve In stature, they said he compared with a pony and his ferocity and courage were in equal measu with his size.

He was identified many times that summe He was often alone, and had a marvellous gift f discovering and avoiding men with bows an arrows. Of these he was afraid ; but for herd men, armed with spears or billhooks, he had utter contempt. He would rush past such hel less guardians, cut down some yearling, ham stringing it first, then later cut its throat. If t herdsmen hurried on with the remaining catt he let them go ; if they strove to fight him o he turned his savage fury on them, and quick claimed one or more of the human victims.

This happened many times that year ; and so the accepted policy of the herdsmen was thi ' Let him have one beef or he will get you ' ; th is, pay toll to the robber, so he may spare yo life.

266

3

Along these lines ran the course of events until late in the summer. The giant wolf had a small band with him at this time, maybe his own brood of the year.

A peasant family named Dubois had a fat sheep that they planned to market in Paris. As winter was far off, the wolves not yet in large packs, and furthermore they could reach Paris by noon if they set out early, the man decided that they would carry the sheep in their one-horse cart, and dispense with any additional protection other than Jean's billhook and a lot of jangling tins, bells, and bird scares that hung from the horse's harness and from the wagonette.

A trip to Paris had its lure in those days as now ; and the wife clamoured to go along. Jean junior, a twelve-year-old boy, also pleaded to go. Thus the three, that is the whole family, the pony and the sheep, set out for Paris on that beautiful September day in 1427.

It proved an eventful occasion ; for the wolf pack that they met was led by the giant wolf. The pony ran away, the sheep was jolted out of the cart and speedily devoured ; then Louha the pony went down, hamstrung and quickly throat-cut. Standing in his cart as his fortress, Jean Dubois made valiant fight with his woodman's billhook, but the wolves were many. It was a short fight, followed by a wild feast ; for these wolves ignored the horse and gorged themselves on the flesh of the human victims.

The loss of a peasant family would not have been considered in itself of vast importance ; but it proved important in that, on that occasion, the giant wolf and his growing brood sampled, proved, and revelled in human flesh. Thence-forth one and all were man-eaters of fanatical obsession.

Not only was the big wolf a man-eater, but his leadership was so forceful that the habit spread ; and in a few months, the dreadful fact was known that the wolves of the Louvre Forest would leave the herd untouched, and feed by preference on the flesh of the human guardians.

The histories of the time reek red with the stories of human slaughter to furnish wolfish feasts. Mostly these tales are given with decoration of horrific adjectives ; but one historian tells us more

exactly that in the first month of that calamitous winter, in the little hollow that lies between the present Montmartre and La Porte Saint Antoine, fourteen persons were killed and devoured by the wolves ; and in each case, the wolves had refused the counter-allurement of beef.

The giant wolf was seen in many of these onslaughts, and was believed to be the instigator of them all. He seemed to possess a charmed life, for all attempts to injure him were vain. There could be no longer any doubt that his head-quarters was Le Louvre. There, close to the Paris gates, he and his bandit crew could at any time attack the coming and going groups of travellers or kine, and boldly take their toll in broad daylight of all who came and went, like a robber baron, or a corsair cruising off the fareway of some great commercial port.

His raids were made by day perforce, for at sunset every gate to the city was shut and kept full barred, with watchmen overhead until the sun arose again. Usually the great wolf shunned the walls and towers, for there were men with crossbows there, and oftentimes they got a wolf. The king wolf himself had been stung, stung just enough to serve him with a warning. And wise was he—one warning was enough.

4

But January, the Snow Moon, came with lessened travel, with herds all housed, with ground game gone. The king wolf's band increased each day ; for, while food was scarce in the far-off hills, there was always promise, rich-smelling promise, of food on the Island burg. Emboldened by hunger and by numbers, the gruesome pack came sneaking, trotting ever nearer to the gates.

Food was scarce in Paris now ; and when a band of cattle was announced as coming fast with mounted guards around them, the city was astir. The great gate at the bridge was thrown wide open, and the beef herd huddled through with every haste. But the wolves had gathered in the rear, gaining courage from their numbers ; and headed by the king wolf, they charged on the wake of the herd.

There was a time of confusion, terror, and stampede. All aimed to reach the shelter of the gate. The cattle went clattering through the main

streets, the foot-folk fled into their homes, the
warders rushed to their towers. The wolves came
surging into the city by the open gate, following
after the beef herd and the guards. There were
some men down, some wolves were pierced by
arrows, a score of officials were yelling their
commands.

Farthest in advance was the king wolf. As the
clattering of chains was heard, men rushed to man
the mighty doors amid the whizzing of arrows,
the battering of hammers, and the tramp of steeds.

' Close the gates ! Trap them ! Quick ! We've
got them ! ' Such were the excited shoutings.

Nothing of that the king wolf understood ; but
when he saw the great gates loosed and swung,
he sensed the trap ; and wheeling at the rear
as he had been at the head of his band, he sprang
through the opening there was still between the
gates, away clear of them. But twenty paces on
was the grim portcullis that gave upon the fareway
of the bridge. His band all cleared it at a dash.
But just as the king wolf passed below, the drop
door flashed and crashed, its sharp edge caught
his tail. But on he went, unhindered and unharmed excepting this :— *his tail was chopped from*

271

his body, was left behind him within the city walls.
Thenceforth, the king wolf had another mark besides his giant form. His tail was gone, all but the
stump ; and thenceforth to all the world he was
known as Courtaud,[1] the King Wolf of the Seine.

5

It was in the early part of the winter of 1428
that Courtaud and his band had made their famous
raid into Paris. That experience had come near
to ending his life, so that thenceforth he was
wary of too near approach to the walls that harboured archers. But the severity of the winter
had four marked results. All cattle remaining
were kept from the fields, and securely housed in
stables where at least they would be warm and
safe from wolves. All gentlefolk for a hundred
miles, if they had the means to travel, were con-
centrating into Paris, to seek the safety of its walls
from pirates, man or wolf. Cattle for food were
daily driven in small, well-guarded. herds to the
city gates. And last, there were ever-growing
packs of wolves in all the woodlands of the Seine.

[1] Bobtail.

Courtaud, the King Wolf of France

As the snow grew deeper and food grew scarcer, the wolves grew more hungry and more daring. A single traveller, yes even a small group of travellers, had no chance of escape if they entered the wolf-infested belt of woods that stretched around Paris.

During all that winter, a state of war existed between the harassed folk of Paris and the ever-hungry wolves. There can be no doubt that hundreds of the weaker and wounded wolves were destroyed and devoured by their stronger brethren. But whatever the loss from this source, it was more than made up by the natural increase ; and, of all the nurseries known, there was none to compare with Le Louvre, the home, the breeding haven of the great king wolf, Courtaud.

Many times was he seen by watchers and by travelling troops of mounted men ; but he seemed immune from all attack, and the terror of his name was on all that part of France. The common salutation of the day to a traveller going forth from Paris to some far point was : ' Well, good-bye ; God bless you, and see that Courtaud does not get you.'

6

The summer of 1428 went by with nothing but the usual toll of cattle, horses and men taken by the bandit wolf who ever lurked near Louvre. That was a year of massacre in all of France— foreign foes, and treacherous rebels nearer home, seemed bent on desolating the whole fair land.

The autumn came with trials ever harder ; and because all food seemed centred now at Paris, the wolves seemed centred all about the Seine. And when the darkest days were on the hills, things grew black dark and ever blacker on the Seine.

From late January to March, the city was in a state of siege, shut up, surrounded by the great king wolf with desperate hungry bands. No man dared venture forth ; and only when the melting snows gave footing for the horses and safety for the mounted men, did a troop of armoured men go forth with orders from the King that brought at laggard length a food supply from far Provence.

As the convoy neared the great Seine gate, the king wolf hung upon the rear, ready for attack ; but warned by bells and trumpets, he held back till the train filed in, the gates were closed, and

the bells of Nôtre Dame pealed joyfully to tell the world, ' Thank God relief has come ! '

7

The summer of 1429 wore on with added horror on the land. War—war—foreign wars—home wars—civil wars and banditry in every region of the land. Grim Death alone was King ; and in whatever form the rulership obtained, it was but another form of death, disease and desolation. Hundreds died that summer to furnish food for the gaunt grey wolves ; and, as a citizen of L'Isle de Seine said grimly in a hopeless jest : ' The fewer mouths there be for us to feed, the better.'

Most of the watchmen in the town, and those who formed the caravan guards, had seen the great king wolf at half a mile. He was plainly marked by his size and his lopped-off tail.

8

At this time, there stood on the south bank of the river, in an angle of the second wall of the city, the Tour de Miel, the city house of a

famous noble family. The Countess of Mi(
though dowager now, was a young and beautif
woman, full of fire, a very Jezebel.

Now, for the furtherance of her pleasures ar
her plans, she had built over the river a galler
a secret passage. One end reached a small incoi
spicuous door outside the wall ; the other reach(
the lady's private room. Midway was a tra
door in the floor, completely hid, but put
operation when a spring was released in the cou
tess's room. Below the trap-door was a chu
bristling with sharp-set knives ; and twenty fe
below was the surging river flood. Many a gallar
it was said, who had not pleased the dame, w
smilingly sent the short and secret way to h
horse safe-tethered near—and never seen again.

Awaiting a lover the high-born lady was, (
that fair moonlight night in the autumn of t
year. Peering from her casement, she saw h
horse approach. Horse, yes—but not a rid(
With sharpened eyes, she peered and watche
The horse seemed small, and came with he:
hung low and cautious step, then left the sen
cover of the trees, and stood in view—a wolf,
monster wolf, a bob-tailed wolf.

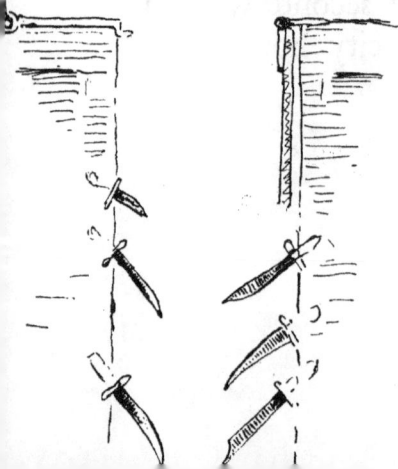

In a flash, the wily dame conceived a plot.
rom the larder, with her own hands, she bore a
aine of beef. She slashed it with a knife to
aultiply its fragrant charm. She tied it with a
ord, and swiftly, silently, threaded the long dark
orridor. The outer door was open wide. She
abbed the threshold with the meat, she dragged
ae bloody mass along to the upper door ; then
·om a peephole, watched.

The great wolf sniffed and sniffed. He cautiously
rew near. He was hungry—he was always
ungry. He revelled in the bloody smell, he
·awled still nearer in and on ; and when the
ountess saw the dim grey bulk had passed into
ae snare, she touched the spring. There was
othing but a click, but that was a warning click.
·he king wolf was alert. In a moment, he sensed
ae trap. Had he gone as he came, he had miser-
bly perished ; but, with one great bound, he
leared the treacherous place, made out the door
ad away, unharmed—and wiser than he ever was
·efore.

9

Then came the hard white months. Christmas that should have smacked of cheer was a time of growing gloom. Plague in the city had laid many a burgher low ; and for lack of better plan, it became the custom to hurl the corpses from the towers that the wolves might feast their fill.

Why this did not spread the plague among the wolves, as fervently was hoped, no man could tell. It seemed to have but two results : it confirmed the wolves in their love for man-meat, and proclaimed the city more than ever a place of feasting and wolf joy.

Since the day when he had been so nearly trapped within the great gate, Courtaud had shunned even the bridge that led to the place. But the deepening snow and ever-scarcer food of the 'Wolf Month' (February) gave ever greater boldness, even rashness, to the wolves.

The siege was on again, much as the winter before, the siege of Courtaud. Almost every day now, the king wolf and his bands were visible from the watch tower—but always out of arrow-shot.

This was another hard winter. The Seine was

278

covered with thick ice ; and often, in the morning, the tracks made it plain that the wolves had taken advantage of this to prowl all around the city walls seeking for some place of possible entry.

But the wall was high and sound ; there was no likelihood of such a visitation ; the watchers hardly tried to follow with the eye these dim grey shades. Beyond taking an occasional chance with bow and arrow in the gloom, the watchers did not seek to harm the wolves upon the ice.

Then something happened.

The Seine was the drainage-water of the Marne, Haute Marne, Laube and Côte d'Or. The winter frost had so much fiercer come on those high hills and mountain plateaux, that all the streams were sealed, the very springs seemed stopped. The water of the Seine, for lack of feeders, fell far below the lowest summer level.

Fronting King Charles's Palace on the river-edge was a landing for his barge. When not in use, this little dock was fenced with an iron gate that dropped a foot below the water-level. But now the level was so lowered that between the grille and the river ice was a three-foot gap.

The prowling wolves found this ; and Courtaud,

heedless of his former evil fortune in the town, assembled a mighty pack. They passed through the gap under the water gate, and by a dozen devious routes appeared in the great Parvis before the Cathedral. A band of holy men were leaving their duties in the chancel to seek their homes, when down on them the wolf band swept. Wholly taken by surprise were the victims, and wholly unarmed. In twenty minutes all were dead. The wolf pack revelled for an hour ; then gorged with human flesh, they fled by the river gap that let them in. Before the terrified burghers could spread the alarm and assemble worth-while help, forty human beings were killed and partly devoured in this dreadful raid. Not a single wolf was slain.

10

That was the crowning feat of the great wolf's life. That was the blackest time in the sad black history of the land. Yet it was but the deeper murk that comes before the dawn.

For a time the city folk of the capital were stunned by the horror of the wolf raid. Many priests and the Archbishop himself were among

the victims. Black, blank despair gripped, paralysed the one who—called the King—should have
risen to leadership in the people's dire distress.
The King was worthy of nothing but contempt.

But brave men there were in abundance in the
streets ; and Boisselier, Captain of the City Guard,
the warden of the town, stood forth undaunted.
His rank gave him no right to speak for all, but
his personal courage and his wisdom did.

' Are Frenchmen down so low, so helpless turned,
that wolves may enter the chief city when they
will, and banquet in the sacred place on human
flesh and blood, and leave unharmed ? This is
their challenge, the challenge I accept. And on
that very spot would I elect to meet the king wolf,
each to each. This is my plan, if you permit,
O King ! '

The weak scared King bowed, trembled, bowed
his head.

And brave Boisselier called the city fathers into
council, and made them see his plan. There were
those who feared and those who scoffed. But the
King had sanctioned the bold attempt. And when
the council ended, Boisselier was given free hand
and full control.

II

Hunter as well as soldier was Boisselier. He
knew the wolf in the woods and he knew the
town. These were the details of his scheme :

For two weeks, no man or beast might leave or
enter Paris ; no garbage be cast over the walls,
so that every source of food should be taken from
the wolves. The iron grille at the King's landing
should be raised and left three feet above the ice
which still was strong, and again at normal level.
All garbage was to be scattered on the Parvis or
square of Nôtre Dame. All beeves that were
killed for food were to be killed in that square,
and the offal scattered about. A high gate or
wall was to be built across all streets leading into
the Parvis ; an open way from the King's landing
to the Parvis, controlled by a gate that could be
closed from an upper window. The entrails of
a beef were to be dragged from the far shore
across the ice to the King's landing, thence up the
alley to the Parvis.

These were the details of Boisselier's trap. And
furthermore, he gave orders that no man might
shoot at the wolves from the walls or shout or

nolest them in any way ; that, so far as possible,
ne city should be silent as a city of the dead.

That very night, the watchers saw the dark
orms of wolves sniffing along the beef trail to
ne barge landing. Yet, strange to say, no wolf
rould enter ; their suspicions were aroused.

After three nights, more wolves came ; and one
r two ventured into the alley as far as the Parvis,
where they fed hastily, then returned. The king
rolf was not with them.

More wolves came as the food supplies outside
ll off—and still more. Then when, at the end
f ten days, the Parvis had been a nightly feasting-
round, Boisselier ordered a kill of twenty beeves
eld in reserve. They were slaughtered in front
f the Cathedral, and the Parvis all around was
olashed with blood and offal. The stench was
rong, far-reaching.

That night, the wolves arrived in force. The
ley from the grille seemed one long and swift
rocession of brown forms. Whether the king
rolf was with them could not be ascertained in
ne dark. The Parvis seemed alive with wolves,
asting, fighting, yelping, grinding bones, and
arling as they fed.

'Twas Boisselier himself who closed the gate, the fateful gate, the one escape. Then all the burgher folk were roused to watch from walls, high roofs, or windows, and wait for the revelation of the coming day.

12

Have ye seen the sun rise back of Nôtre Dame over the far east river stretch? Then have ye seen the glory of a miracle. It is a scene that never fails to thrill.

And yet there never was before or since so weird and wild and thrillsome a scene as that which met the burghers' eyes that morning when the city sent its all to see. Crowded on the roofs, the upper windows, convenient walls, were men and women, nobles and peasants, eager, anxious, triumphant, acclamant. And in the broad Parvis below were scores and scores of grim brown wolves, trapped, prisoned, trapped, all felons doomed to die.

Some were racing and leaping up against the pitiless walls, hoping for escape. Some were hiding, skulking in corners, or in the arches of

the great façade. Some were fighting with each other. Some were lying sullen in defiant ease. And there, stalking calmly past them all, sniffing and peering at the entering gate, was Courtaud, the dread king wolf.

As the sun rose on the stirring scene, a great murmur spread among the human watchers. The murmur rose to a shout, wild *vivas!* rent the morning mists. Then, on the roof of the sacristy by the church appeared the white-robed choir, and *Te Deum* was sung for the amplitude of victory.

Then Boisselier gave the word, and archers from every vantage-point let fly their winged shafts. Wolf after wolf went down ; but few fell struck by a single bolt. The wounded were more than the dead, and many a wolf drew with his teeth the shaft and then renewed the hopeless fight. Even the poor weak King was filled with sporting fire, and twanged his bow till all his shafts were flown.

And still the wolves raced round. Scores were dead before an hour had passed. Many more were wounded, and a great brown mass was surging round untouched.

And Courtaud—where was he ?

In the centre of the square is the fountain, a broad basin carried on four high pillars of stone. Here plainly to be seen was the king wolf, calmly lying on the ground under the bowl, perfectly pro-tected from arrow or any other missile. Nothing of the massacre going on escaped him, yet he did not move or seem affected by the roar.

Behind him, protected by the pillars, were other wolves, and a careful glance showed that in the three arches of Nôtre Dame were groups of wolves who found in them protection from the shafts.

It was nearly noon when the last of the racing wolves was downed. The ground was brown with them ; they were in hundreds. The massacre seemed over, but still the great king wolf was there unharmed, and a handful with him, and others in the porches—half a hundred it seemed in all.

Then Boisselier stood up and called his guards about him, and thus he said :

' God has given us a tremendous victory. He has delivered our enemies into our hands. Here have we trapped and slain them in hundreds. But the greatest and fiercest of the wolves is still unharmed ; he crouches there where arrow cannot reach him.

' He sent to me his challenge when first he entered here ; to me, the Captain of the City Guard. I accepted his challenge ; and now, as warrior meeting worthy foe, I must go in and fight him to the death. Nevertheless, because there are yet a score of wolves to meet, I will take with me a score of fighting men. At least our King shall see a fight.'

Hundreds there were who volunteered. But Boisselier was a sportsman ; he sought for something like a fair fight. He picked a score of stalwarts who were skilled with sword and spear. Descending by ladders into the arena, they formed in line before the King's window ; there made salute, then faced about and marched on the sullen foe.

Then a strange thing came about. Acting on orders from the King, the chief huntsman opened a side door ; and, blowing his horn, marched in, while a pack of great wolfhounds came belling on the scene. They were equal in numbers to the wolves, and fired by the excitement and the support of all around, were keen for fight.

'Keep back!' shouted Boisselier to his men.
'At least the Court shall see a fight to-day, shall
have a chance to measure dog and wolf.'

Then came a scene that all the world would
thrill to see. The king wolf rose, gave one great
gathering howl, the war-cry of his race; and at
the dogs they went. The battle lasted half an
hour, and every dog went down. Great Courtaud
slew a dozen in that fray. And not a wolf was
slain; but few were hurt.

'Good!' said Boisselier. 'Now it is our turn.'

And the valiant guardsmen charged. Wolf after
wolf went down, for the spears were long and
sharp. But many men were hurt, and five went
down, throat-slashed.

Cheers from the crowded roofs and the royal
banner waving inspired the men. They pushed
the fight. With their long lances, they reached
under the fountain; they speared the wolves,
they killed near all. But some, with Courtaud
in the lead, broke away and dashed for another
haven, the doorway of the church. Here, under
the stone arcade, they faced about—Courtaud and
five—with a ring of men around them. A mauling gruelling fight—men slashed in limb and neck.

288

Wolf after wolf went down, till only one was left—the great grim king.

Then Boisselier, a valiant man, a lover of an even fight, cried out:

'Hold back! Since only he is left and challenged me, we'll settle this in single fight.' And charged with his lance as knight against a knight.

The great wolf reared and sprang to meet him; the lance went through his chest. But he sprang with all his force, slid up the lance, and the man went down. And Courtaud, with his fearful slashing fangs, cut through the leather jerkin, ripped the throat-strap of his helm, and tore his throat out as he lay. Down, down, they fell at grips, their red lives gushed, the great grim wolf and the brave strong man. They lay in death together.

13

Now did the great Cathedral chimes peal out, a merry peal, then a tolling dirge. Then *Gloria in Excelsis* rang from the church chimes. The crowd came leaping over the barricades. The wolves, three hundred, were laid down in rows. And

high on a red-and-black draped catafalque was
Courtaud laid, high in the air where all could see.

And the herald blared his trumpet 'fore the King,
and cried aloud to all the world :

> *Courtaud is dead !*
> *The great grim Wolf is fallen !*
> *Come all and see.*
> *His reign is over !*
> *God has remembered His people !*
> *Come and see !*

And all the world filed past to see, to see with
their own eyes, that Courtaud sure was dead.

Sad tribute too was paid to gallant Boisselier,
the deliverer. But the world was all rejoicing.

This was the beginning of the glad new day for
France. Even then, the God-sent Maid was at
Orleans. And what Boisselier did for the Paris
wolves, the heaven-born Maid was soon to do for
the English wolves.

The new fair day had come for France, at cost
of noble sacrifice.

XVIII

The Leopard Lover

'The Leopard Lover' has a unique history. About fifty years ago, I read of a strange adventure in the desert—the friendly association of a lost soldier and a Leopard. It made a deep impression on me.

I tried to find it recently, but could not place it by title or by author. So I rewrote it from memory as 'The Leopard Lover'. Then, after my version was complete, I rediscovered the story. It was Honoré de Balzac's 'Passion in the Desert'. My rendering, however, had so little resemblance to that of Balzac, excepting in the main thought, that, with apologies to the distinguished Frenchman, I have decided to publish my own version.

HE was a rugged old French soldier who told me this tale. His countenance was seamed and blotched with weather brunt, his broad shoulders were rounded, he lacked an arm, and one leg was a-limp. But his eyes, those windows of the soul, were ablaze with the courage and steadfastness that must have made of him an ideal soldier some fifty years ago. There was dignity and simplicity in his manner ; and when I looked upon his strong and kindly face I knew that he was telling me the truth.

From Provence he came ; and had joined the standard of Napoleon in that ill-fated foray on the Upper Nile. Twenty-two years of age he was then ; and, as he said it, I pictured him to myself, a very Adonis.

And then I played a crafty game. I ordered *vin champagne*. Oh ! how it plays on the chords of life, how it unlooses the tongue, and stirs the memory harp.

I was not wrong. And this, the tale, I tell it as it came to me.

I was young then and impulsive. I was suffering from a cruel disappointment in love. So I joined the Army ; for the magic name of Bonaparte was there to win the adoration of all strong and valiant men. Away to the land of the Sphinx we sailed, and I was not a little dashed to find myself enrolled, not in Napoleon's own command, but that of

General Desaix, whose job it was to raid the Upper Country.

But the Magraubin Arabs, mounted every man on a fleet steed, and at home in the sandy wastes, were a very different proposition to the dull and sedentary Fellaheen along the Nile. They swooped down on us at unexpected times, and drove off our camels, harried our support when we were weak ; or, if we rallied in force, they swept away on their desert steeds like the desert wind itself in a baffling storm of sand and dust.

I was on outpost duty when they came one night. The rest of our vedettes were killed, and I made prisoner. Bound on a baggage mule, they bore me off. And, when two long days' march away, and far beyond the chance of my reprieve, they halted in an oasis of palms about a spring ; each and every man, and every horse, worn out. And there they slept.

Not a sentry was posted—not one Arab was on watch that night. Escape was my fierce impelling thought ; that kept me watchful. My hands and feet were bound with cords ; and when I saw the sodden sleep of deep exhaustion on the band, I wriggled to the nearest of my sleeping

293

captors. With my teeth I drew his scimitar, and
with infinite silent pains got it between my knees.
On this I sawed the cords that bound my hands.
Thus free, I cut the bindings of my feet, and stood
erect.

In the dim starlight, I moved with speed and
silence, secured a rifle, a scimitar, and a dagger,
with plenty of ammunition, also a bag of oats and
a sack of dried dates.

The horses were tethered about. All were
noble brutes, so I took the first ; and, mounting
swiftly and silently, sped away. I began at a
walking speed for silence ; but once we were
well away I plied the spur, and we galloped and
galloped—a glorious gallop—for freedom was in
sight.

There was no moon that night, the north star
was hidden in a haze. We soldiers are not much
on astronomy, but I felt sure that such and such
a blazing star was the Morning Star, the star that
marked the east. And knowing that my people
in any force were far away to the east, I kept
my steed's head that way, and rode and spurred
and rode. That star became my guide.

At length, my star was setting far ahead, and

for some strange reason that I did not understand there was a streak of light along the other world rim, far behind me.

Alas for my poor wit! That star was Venus in the *western* sky. I often wondered if it was mere chance, or was it that Venus was my lodestar, the true star of my soul.

I had not spared myself or my horse. He was far too slight for my weight. His efforts were overmuch; his gallop had died away. He was down to a dragging, stumbling march; and just as the stars had faded from the sky, the poor brute fell and rose no more.

As I sat sorrowful and despairing beside him, the day dawned fully. The sun came up on the *wrong side of my world*, and I was dumbfounded, more than ever in despair. For it meant I had not travelled toward my people, but farther and farther into the far vast sea of sand.

As I scanned the offing in blank hopelessness, I noted in the morning light a faint far fringe of trees—palm trees, maybe, but many miles away. With all weapons and my food, I now set out on foot to reach the promised haven.

Although it seemed but a few miles, I was all day trudging through the weary sand before I reached the beckoning trees. Just as the sun went down, I arrived. The little group of trees proved a grove of several hundred beautiful date palms, strewn along the banks of a hollow that in the middle made a lower depth in which was a sparkling spring.

I put forth my last remaining strength, and reached the spring—and drank—oh, what a glorious life-giving draught it was ! And then, in a rocky hollow, wind-worn to the shape of a cradle, I slept the sleep of utter weariness.

I was awakened by the sun ; though not yet high, its heat was intense, and my rocky couch had by chance no shelter in or near it.

As I stood on this little eminence, I had an all too comprehensive view of the awful world about me. The desert—terrible, majestic—rolled away on all sides like a fiery sea, or a shining mirror of steel, with varying flashing lakes over which a mist of fire was drifting and swirling in the endless windrift that at times might well engender—often did—the dread simoom. And the heightening sun showered down its mist of fire till coppery vault and red-brown sand were fused and mingled, fearsome, deadly.

I shouted aloud to reassure myself, but the hollowness of sky and scene seemed to swallow up the sound, and I found no echo but the mockery in my own sad heart.

I went at noon to the spring for a drink, and as I drew near saw a small band of desert antelope. They also found in this their water-supply, and they scurried off. After quenching my thirst, I looked well about, and descried not only the tracks of antelope and many small creatures of the desert, but also the unmistakable marks of some large beast of prey. Whether lion, cheetah, or leopard, I could not quite be sure. But I took the warning, and set about making for myself a night shelter that should be some protection; for alas, I had no means of making a fire, and I knew not how long I might have to sojourn there.

I worked all day at my cabin, hacking down some of the smaller palms with my scimitar, and dragging them as well as a great pile of loose stones to the place selected. I had the walls of a low cabin built as well as a strong roof of palm trunks thatched with the broad leaves before night came. And, after a meal of dates and water, I lay down in my new abode, and slept the sound sleep of utter tiredness that is the heritage of manly youth rejoicing in putting forth its manly strength.

I had made provision for a doorway, but no window. The cabin was about my own length, and half of it taken up with the bed bunk of palm leaves that I had made.

In the middle of the night I was wakened by a singular and portentous sound. It was like a growl, and yet in some sort a snore. But it came from lungs of larger power and force than ever human had.

I felt my hair rising with terror as I remembered the tracks I had seen by the spring. Whatever the creature was, it was now lying near or in the entrance of my hut. I rose on my elbow, and slowly made out in the gloom a huge, dark form ; and near one end of it, two dull green-yellow lights. At first I thought it some weird hallucination in my brain ; but I swung my head a little and held very still. The lights rose higher, but kept the same distance apart. The snoring

298

sound ceased, or rather changed into a deep rumbling; and at that moment, a pungent, searching animal smell came in a sort of fog-wave, so it filled my hut. And now I fully knew I was trapped in my own dwelling by some huge beast of prey. What, I could not tell. But the creature had me, and was watching me; and the rumble was the angry warning growl of a beast that knows it has me in its power.

I had my rifle as well as my side-arms, and I braced myself with the grim thought : ' Well, I won't be taken without a fight.' Had there been light enough, I would have invited a finish right now, but the gloom was impenetrable to me, though little handicap to the beast. I knew that if I merely wounded with my shot, the creature would make short work of me. Since I could wait, I waited; and, in the gloom, I felt unceasingly the peering watchfulness of those blazing night-seeing eyes.

At last the moon rose, and turned its tropic splendour on the scene. In its waxing light, I clearly made out the long, lithe spotted form of a leopard, splendid in its catlike beauty, fearsome in its size.

I was trained in the short-arms for a close fight, and slowly drew my scimitar as more dependable than the gun. But the roof was too low for a swing; there was not room to stand up, and the scimitar is a poor tool for a thrust. The creature was not within reach, and would be amply warned if I tried to rush forward. No, clearly it was my plan to wait, if possible, for full day; then rely on one shot from my gun.

At last, the day dawned, and I could examine my enemy at ease—an unusually fine big leopard, with smears of fresh blood on muzzle, paws, and snowy throat. 'Well,' I thought, 'it has recently had a good dinner, so won't be so very hungry. That argues a little respite for me.'

When at length, and rather lazily, the leopard arose, it swung its head in a somewhat languid style, gave its great tail an upward curl, then leaned against the sidepost of my door, and rubbed its neck as a cat might rub against a chair.

And now I had a chance for fuller observation. Though so large, it was a female; the fur on her throat, breast and belly was snowy white, beautifully decorated with jet-black spots like charcoal lumps in swansdown. The spots on her legs

300

made rosettes like bracelets of blackest velvet
sheen. Her over-robe was of golden-tan, short
and glossy, and everywhere embellished with
rosettes of velvety black. From each side of her
mouth there sprang, like two bright silver sprays,
the whiskers, white and tactile. And deep in the
broad brow above were the blazing jewels of her
eyes—amethyst, topaz at times, but always with a
glint of opalescent fire.

She was beautiful, and gave no hint of menace.
But she looked so cruel, I knew she could be a
perfect devil of ferocity if aroused.

'Well,' I thought, 'it is your life or mine.
Each of us is awaiting the proper moment of
attack.'

And slowly I swung my rifle in line for her
heart. I felt I had her in my power ; and yet I
could not pull. She swung still nearer, and rubbed
her shoulder on the doorside. I braced myself for
a finish. She turned her blazing eyes upon me—
yellow-green in the glint of her gold-brown hair
—and in a flash an ancient memory gripped me.

I had a sweetheart once ; a composite of joyous
fairy and remorseless fiend, a very tigress. She
was beautiful as she was wilful ; her hair was

301

red-gold, and her eyes the green topaz gems that go with such a chevelure. She was beautiful ; she was winsome. But she was insanely jealous and cruel—more cruel than a vampire. More than once she had threatened me with a knife. I loved her to distraction ; but she crucified me, then threw me down in scorn. I joined the Army ; and in a week she killed herself. Yes, that was the end of my blazing fiery Mignonne. She sent after me a little word : ' Good-bye, we shall meet again.'

She had been my dream princess for long, and ever she haunted my dreams. And, as I gazed at this beautiful beast before me, with the gold-red hair and the red-gold eyes, I felt the pang of an old sad love—a dead love that was not dead.

The leopard turned those jewel eyes on me ; there was no menace ; there was understanding, there was love. I gasped, I could not help it : ' Mignonne ! '

I do not pretend that she understood the word, but my intonation was kind and inviting. She glided into my cabin, and as she rubbed her back and neck against my knees, in catlike amoration, I laid my rifle down and stroked her head, her neck, her back. She vibrated with a quick electric

ock, and rubbed against my hand—and purred ;
rred with a long low purr, the purr that in the
orld of cats means love. 'I love you, I invite
ur love.'
From that time on, she gave me every evidence
affection, following me about, rubbing against
y legs, inviting my caresses. Yet I had moments
hen I felt that this was nothing but the prelude
a deadly attack—the cat-play with a mouse
at is easily in its power when the time comes
destroy it.
That very afternoon, a huge vulture alighted
ot far from the spring. I drew nearer, cautiously,
r a better view, when suddenly the Leopard
dy rushed ahead and faced me with an angry
owl, an unmistakable expression of fury in her
ce, her eyes, her manner.
'Oho !' I thought, 'my lady is jealous.' I
cked off, and returned to our hut, where at
ce she resumed her kittenlike play.
The night passed as before. She mounted guard
pposite my bed. For a time in the night she
as absent, but at sunrise she was back.
During these days, I suspected that she was
eding on the carcass of my dead horse. Her

line of travel, the traces on her face and snowy fur, seemed to justify that idea. It may have been so at first, but there were other supplies in reach.

On the third morning when I arose she was away, but speedily appeared, carrying a fine fat antelope, evidently her own kill. She laid it at my feet, and purred and frolicked. I set about skinning the quarry. She watched the process with intense eye, and when I divided the carcass, she set about her meal, growling not a little, and licking the still warm flesh.

I had no liking for raw meat, but many times in the Army we have jerked our extra supply, that is, cut it in thin strips, and let it dry in the sun. So treated, it lasts a long time, and is good to eat without further preparation.

I had cut up the meat, when it occurred to me to turn the skin to account. I saw in this a possible water-bottle for use when next I should travel. I filled the skin with sand, and tied it in bottle shape with a strip of the hide. The leg skins furnished neck-straps ; and when the skin was dry, I emptied out the sand, and now had a water-tight bag.

My companion watched the whole process without expressing any emotion. But later I undertook something else that had a different effect. Ever the thought of escape or rescue was with me; and in furtherance of such a possibility, I determined to sacrifice my red shirt. I climbed a tall palm tree with much difficulty, and from its highest stalk I hung my shirt as a signal flag. My Leopard lady watched me with intense gaze, growled a little; and as soon as I had come down she scrambled quickly up, struck the flagstaff a fierce blow that sent it tumbling to earth, then as quickly came down.

Now we began to understand each other. Each day our friendship grew. I found I could always win her active favour by stroking her back, her head, her face. She loved the friendly hand touch; and after a few strokes would rub her head against me, loudly purring, or roll on the ground at my feet in an ecstasy of pleasure.

The fear that she meant to kill me died away in a few days. After two weeks, we were close friends, daily and hourly companions. She procured her own meat and drink, and offered me a share. With plenty of dates, dried meat and

water, I was faring well. I felt more and more
that back of those jewel eyes was a soul—the
soul of a woman ; and I called her ever oftener
' Mignonne '.

Sometimes in the morning she was absent
from our hut ; but the long loud call ' Mignonne '
never failed to bring her bounding, joyously bounding. We surely were friends, ever nearer and
dearer. The thought of killing her, or the fear
of her killing me, died wholly away. We were
frank and equal partners in our desert lives.

But the hope of rejoining my own people would
not die. And I prepared for a dash by storing
up dried meat and dates. On a given night, I
filled my water-bag, and hung it outside my hut.

As was her habit, she rose before dawn, and
disappeared. I knew she would be gone at least
an hour. So I hung the water-bag around my
neck by the two thong straps crossing my breast,
seized my food and weapons, and set out as fast
as I could silently travel toward the east, where
in three or four days I hoped to find my people.

I was possessed of a whirl of thoughts that
soon amounted to a delirium—hope to escape—
fear of pursuit and vengeance—determination to

fight for freedom—and not a little remorse—a tender thought for the bright-eyed queen of the desert who had saved me and loved me.

The sun rose and I was blindly dashing on, exhausting myself unneedfully ; glancing forward for a sign of hope, and backward for a cause of fear. I was crossing a rocky escarpment when, at its farther side, I lost my footing and was hurled down a long granite cleft into a thorny thicket, stunned, torn and bleeding ; and hanging, as it seemed when I came to, by the thongs of my water-bag that had caught in the cleft of a strong acacia crotch. I was absolutely helpless. How long I was there, I do not know. But an hour after I came to my senses, I heard a loud harsh roar, and in a flash my Leopard lady came bounding over the rocks.

Her countenance was distorted with fury. She stood above me and roared and growled. I called out feebly ' Mignonne ! ' In a moment, she was by my side ; the anger faded from her face and voice. She sprang up the thorny trunk, tore loose the thongs of the water-bottle about it. This let me drop ; then following, she dragged me out of that rocky trap, out on to the smooth sand.

I drank deeply of the water. She lapped a little ; then, in a rage, she tore the water-skin to useless shreds.

She waited near. I recovered enough to stroke her head in token of gratitude, and a plea for forgiveness. I was under no doubt as to which way I should travel now ; and back to our oasis I trudged with my wild beast-love beside me.

We were all day getting back ; but there were food and rest awaiting.

It was fully three days before I recovered. She had watched by my bed. She brought me game as she killed it. But I had to crawl to the spring when I needed water. I no longer had any doubt of the deep affection of my desert love. And not the least evidence of that was the furious jealousy at any hint of the love bond breaking. I was ashamed of my own perfidy, and yet my heart kept harking back to my own people. The longing to rejoin them was overwhelming.

Mignonne was off on her breakfast quest one day, when I set about a new scheme. From the edge of my red shirt I tore a long strip. In each end of this I fastened a stone. Tied in the middle of it, but loosely rolled and bound, as a package,

I placed a sleeve of the red shirt. Then, after many
attempts, I threw this into the top of a slim palm
near the crest of the hill. Like bolas, the stones
lapped around the palm branch, and hung. It
was not long before the breeze reopened the
package, and my red sleeve flag was flaunting.

When my Leopard lover came home, she found
me in the hut. But soon her eye caught the red
flag a-flutter. She eyed it suspiciously, walked
around the tree, and smelt at the trunk, convinced herself that I had not been up, and gradually got used to the signal flag. Several times in
the days that followed I saw her regarding it
with interest and suspicion, but at last it was
ignored.

Two months in all had gone, and still I was a
prisoner with my desert queen. Never in my life
had I seen a more beautiful creature ; beautiful
in anger, or in sleep, but perfectly glorious in
play. I had learned to love her deeply and sin-
cerely. And, though I still looked forward to
the day of escape, it was not without a sense of
pain, a knowledge that for me, as for her, it would
be a fearful wrench—an agony of sorrow, maybe
a death agony.

Mignonne was off on some expedition one day when I strolled to the hilltop on which stood the tree that bore my flag. Far over the sands I saw a low dark cloud of dust. It grew quickly bigger, and now I knew that horsemen were approaching. Who ? Arab foemen, or brethren from France ? I hurried back to my hut to secure my weapons, and discreetly to hide.

The band came quickly on. Then I knew that they had sighted my red flag. Closer they came, and now I could dimly discern the uniform of France.

They slowed up, came at a walk, closely watching the flag, and scrutinizing every hollow that might hide a foe.

My soul was ablaze ; I stepped forward with a cry of greeting. But in an instant, I was face to face with Mignonne. A raging fiend, she stood between, her tusks were gleaming, her face contorted ; and in her chest a thunder growl that shook her form. I tried to pass her. She reared on her hind legs, a paw on each of my shoulders ; and, as I gazed into her fiery eyes, I knew I was looking into the eyes of a woman, jealous-mad.

She struck my face with her paw, a cruel blow,

a blow that drew the blood. I jerked my rifle into line for her heart—and *fired*.

She gave a long and agonizing scream, then backward fell. Oh, that scream ! that woman scream ! I dropped my gun, and fell on my knees beside her. She was moaning now. I cried aloud : ' Mignonne ! Mignonne ! Forgive ! Forgive me ! '

She tried to rise, but her life was ebbing. She reached her snowy muzzle and licked my face and hands, and moaned. I knew she moaned : ' Good-bye.'

I was mad with sorrow now ; I could only wail : ' Mignonne ! Mignonne ! My loved Mignonne ! Farewell, but we shall meet again— M-i-g-n-o-n-n-e ! '

And the soldiers found us lying there together.

XIX

Who were the Heroes?

WHEN DARWIN published his epoch-marking *Origin of Species* in 1859, the whole world of science and religion was in an uproar. The fact that he was leading mankind in a march toward the light was nothing compared with the horror of disturbing existing notions and conditions.

There was no limit to the reprobation of this new prophet by folk already lined up with the ancient way. All attempts to refute his ideas by hurling hard facts were worse than futile ; all proved boomerangs and recoiled on the attacking party till their total defeat was accomplished.

Darwin's scientific triumph was complete. The religious people retired into their dogmas, sullen, defiant ; but really defeated, though raising feeble shouts of ' We win '.

But the sentimental people had to be dealt with. The horrible idea of saying that man is

akin to monkeys ! Actually a blood relation !
Shocking ! Loathsome !

To the scientists, Darwin gave a scientific answer ;
and now, to the sentimentalists, he responded with
a sentimental reply. He told them three historic
tales, which carried their own lesson :

I

When Bruce, the famous African traveller,
marched through Abyssinia, in the last part of the
eighteenth century, he was accompanied by a
caravan of bearers, soldiers, coolies, hunters, &c.,
and a multitude of dogs. As they entered a rocky
valley, they surprised a band of baboons feeding
in the open. A rabble of dogs and hunters gave
chase. The baboons scrambled up the rocks, and
soon found safety on a high crag—all but one, a
baby baboon. He thought he had found a short
cut of his own, and scrambled up a near jutting
point, which proved to be an outlying rock.

In a moment, he was surrounded by the pack
of dogs, leaping up at him and hoping speedily
to tear him to pieces, for he was but a few feet
above them.

In his dire extremity, the little baboon raised the scream for help that is part of the baboon vocabulary. The troop of his relatives high on the crag wheeled about, and uttered a chorus of the loud coughing barks that is their own war-cry. For a minute they glared and barked.

Then their leader, a grand old warrior, swung from the cliff, came galloping toward the pack of hounds, smashed right and left among them— tore, wrenched, and slashed with his four great paws and his mighty jaws, till they recoiled a little ; then through the gap and over the wounded he sprang and scrambled up the low point that harboured the baby baboon.

Here he rested a few moments, carefully poised the baby on the back of his neck, took a deep breath, and sprang again among the howling dogs. Down and up and over he smashed and tore. Many a cut from fierce strong jaws he got ; but his courage, his strength, his marvellous tusks carried him through. The rabble, fifty strong, was beaten back, and the glorious old hero reached the cliff and scrambled up to safety, wounded, winded, bleeding, but undismayed, with the baby quite unhurt.

That was Story No. 1, a true story, a noble truth.

2

In the London Zoo, in the biggest monkey cage, were different species and many individuals, among them a little Macaque, a small creature from Africa, and also a Chacma, a fierce, big baboon from the same country.

The little monkey had been taken ill, but was carefully nursed by the keeper and brought through safely. Thenceforth, he felt for the keeper the deepest affection. The feeling was mutual ; they were devoted friends.

Once a week, the keeper had to enter the cage for a general clean-up ; and, acting on the warning of those who knew the baboon, he always had with him a short heavy fork with sharp steel prongs.

The baboon knew right well what this was for, and what it could do. He held it in wholesome dread ; and as soon as the keeper entered, armed with the fork, he would retreat to the highest perch, muttering savage threats in his deep chest,

316

chopping his fearful tusks like a wild boar, and glaring unutterable hate at the keeper.

Many weeks had passed with no other demonstration. But one day the keeper, grown careless, left his pike at one corner of the big cage ; and, plying his broom, worked ever farther from it, till it was quite beyond his reach. The baboon had ceased his noisy threats, and now was glaring in silent hate, intent on a plan.

As the keeper passed heedlessly under the baboon, the latter leaped. He landed on the man's shoulders, dashed him to the ground, face downwards ; and, in a moment, those awful jaws had closed on the neck of the unprotected man. He was beyond human help.

But, like a flash, the tiny Macaque sprang to the rescue. He was terribly afraid of the great Chacma —but his friend was in danger.

With a warlike scream, he sprang on the huge brute's face, dug every claw he could into the monster's eyes, tore with his teeth, attacked the only spot that he could harm ; and ceased not screaming for any—every—help at hand.

The baboon let go the man to save his own eyes. The keeper sprang to his feet, secured the spear, and drove the four-legged demon to his perch.

But alas, too late ! The tiny monkey had received his death wound ; and, sobbing, clinging to the keeper's hand, his little frame a-shake, he slowly sank. The keeper kissed his little friend as he would a baby's face—and the brave little life went out.

That is Story No. 2 ; and verily it is a truth, for I myself did see on the man the long-healed wounds that the Chacma's fangs had given.

3

When Lord Byron went around the world in the early part of the nineteenth century, he called at Tierra del Fuego, the extreme southern part of South America ; and there had many chances to see the squalid native men and their squalid way of life.

He saw a huge, strong human brute climb a cliff, and there gather a small basketful of sea-birds' eggs, perhaps the favourite food of the tribe. He saw the savage hand it to a little boy, his son, to carry to the camp where others of the family were assembled.

On some wet rocks the child's foot slipped, the eggs were spilled, and all were broken.

With a bellow of animal rage at the loss of his food, the big brute sprang on his son, seized him by the feet, and smashed his head and body down on a rock, then flung the mangled form to one side.

The child's mother came timorously running, picked up the quivering little body, bent her naked breast over it as it lay on her knees, and moaned— and moaned. The big brute gave a growl of anger, and set off in search of more eggs.

'My God !' said Byron, as he gazed in horror from afar. 'This is a human being.'

'Now,' said Darwin, after reciting these three absolutely truthful accounts. 'You sentimentalists who recoil in horror when I tell you that you and the monkeys are akin. With which of these three would you most proudly claim relationship ? The heroic old baboon who would leave a place of safety, and come at peril of his own life against overwhelming numbers to the rescue of a little one that maybe was not his own, but merely one of his tribe in desperate peril, screaming in fear of its life ; and the brave little Macaque that set love for his friend above fear for himself, and rescued the keeper at cost of his own life ? Or would you rather claim as a kinsman the beastly brute of a savage who would kill his own little son for the sake of a few sea-birds' eggs ?

'I know what my choice would be, and I doubt not that the same would hold with all who hearken to the tales and keep an open mind.'

www.ingramcontent.com/pod-product-compliance
Lightning Source LLC
Chambersburg PA
CBHW020524270326
41927CB00006B/434